Women workers in the Sri Lanka
plantation sector

Women, Work and Development, 5

Women workers in the Sri Lanka plantation sector

An historical and contemporary analysis

Rachel Kurian

International Labour Office   Geneva

ISBN 92-2-102992-1
ISSN 0253-2042

First published 1982
Second impression 1985

Printed in Switzerland

Preface

The World Employment Conference in June 1976 noted that women constitute the group at the bottom of the ladder in many developing countries, in respect of employment, poverty, education, training and status.   Concerning rural women, the Conference recommended that measures be taken to relieve their work burden and drudgery by improving working and living conditions, as well as by providing more resources for investment.   In 1979, the Advisory Committee on Rural Development urged the ILO to continue and extend its work concerning women in rural development, with a special focus on women in the disadvantaged groups.

The ILO's Programme on Rural Women, which is part of the ILO's World Employment Programme, attempts to translate these recommendations into action.   In view of the inadequate research done on employment patterns and labour processes, poverty and organisations of rural women, the main focus of the Programme has been on studies and field research subcontracted to experts in the Third World. The general approach of the Programme is to move gradually from a substantial conceptual and information base to the dissemination and exchange of information and insights through seminars and workshops, followed by the planning and implementation of technical cooperation projects to assist the poorest strata among rural women, in close consultation, where possible, with rural women's own organisations.

The present study examines the nature and evolution of the plantation system in Sri Lanka, with a particular focus on its implications for women workers.   It highlights the difficulties which remain even after the workers become organised and the sector regulated in this particular case (which of course is not unique to Sri Lanka, to plantations or to the developing world).   Lower earnings, inadequate access to child care facilities and incredibly long work days are among women's most serious problems.

The situation of women plantation workers in Sri Lanka reflects a phenomenon prevalent to varying degrees in most societies - male domination and discrimination against women.   This inevitably shows up in many aspects of a society, such as places of work and organisations, including trade unions.   There is, however, growing attention

being paid - most importantly by women workers themselves in many
societies (including Sri Lanka) to reducing such inequality at
different levels.

Since 1950, with the establishment of the Committee on Work on
Plantations, the ILO has been continuously acting on behalf of plantation workers.   This Committee has adopted several comprehensive
resolutions and conclusions covering various aspects of social
policy and workers' protection;   in particuar, in 1971, the Committee adopted at its sixth session conclusions concerning conditions
of work of women and young workers in plantations.   The plantation
sector is also covered by two major international instruments
adopted by the ILO, namely the Plantations Convention and Recommenda-
tion, 1958 (No. 110);   these are to be revised during the 1982
International Labour Conference.

While there are a number of elements specific to plantations
in each country and to particular crops (for example, the way in
which the creation of plantations affected the local economy and
population), plantation systems seem to have similarities across
crops and cultures.   Additional research on women in plantation
systems is planned, to document further the nature of the labour
process on plantations and to form the basis for a comparative
analysis.

Dharam Ghai,
Chief,
Rural Employment Policies Branch,
Employment and Development Department.

Author's note

   This study set out to examine the nature and situation of
female labour on Sri Lanka's plantations.   It aimed to analyse the
different activities undertaken by the female worker and the implications of these for the plantation sector and for the economic
development of the country as a whole.   It intended to analyse the
various forces which shaped the position in which these women found
themselves, and to ask how these forces had been changing over time.
It was hoped from this to come to a better understanding of the
options open to the Sri Lankan Government in developing the plantation sector as a dynamic and viable element in the national economy
and in bettering the position of female workers who comprised a very
large part of this labour force.

   At the same time, it was also quite evident that the position
of the female worker, or of labour in general, could not be appreciated without a clear understanding of the nature and development
of these plantations as a specific form of agrarian organisation,
or of the plantation community as a political force.   Many of the
principal structural features that were to be observed had their
roots in the early slave plantations of the fifteenth century;   they
had emerged in response to particular economic needs, and they had
since become an intrinsic part of the plantation system.

   A crucial part of this was labour organisation.   As a response
to the manpower needs of the nineteenth century the planters in
Sri Lanka deliberately imported labour and created a "foreign",
immigrant enclave community using its traditional social structure
as a means of control.   To some extent it employed labour from
nearby villages, but this was by no means the major part of its
labour supply.   The wider social background of this labour
was, and still is, of considerable importance in analysing labour
practices and labour control.   These concerns are reflected in the
first parts of this study which examine the evolution of the plantation system, the specific case of Sri Lanka, and the kinship relations and traditional norms and values of its labour force.   In
this particular attention is paid to the position of women.

Turning to the contemporary situation, it was also quite clear that the plantation sector as such was extremely important for the future stability and growth of the Sri Lankan economy. The three main plantation crops - tea, rubber and coconuts - together comprised over 90 per cent of the country's agricultural exports and 70 per cent of its total exports by value. There was no doubt that they played a very crucial role in its economic development. At the same time, the state plantations were by far the largest employer, and the fate of the country and the fate of this labour force were in many obvious and subtle ways intertwined. What is more, over half of this labour force was female. The needs of these women seemed to be very important and to form an integral part of the future development of these estates.

In recent years the plantation sector has been faced with mounting labour problems. The trade unions have been pressing for significant improvements in income and in working conditions. At the same time, the industry has been facing a number of organisational difficulties in the wake of the Land Reform Acts of 1972 and 1975 and a decline in the world market value of its export crops. In this context the viability of the industry has become problematic.

It is clear that the present situation of the female worker cannot continue as it is indefinitely. Both management and the trade unions are already quite aware of many of the inequalities that are inherent in the plantation system as it is today, and especially of the wage differentials and differences in the hours and conditions of work between men and women. They are also aware that the housing, medical, welfare and other facilities available to their workers are often inadequate, and that these tend to affect women rather more than men.

The economic viability of the estates is obviously an important factor that has to be borne in mind in discussing the possibilities of change in these dimensions. However, the worker's situation has in many ways deteriorated to such a level that serious efforts have to be made to bring about change. Programmes have been introduced to this effect, and some improvements have indeed been implemented. Nevertheless, these efforts have been very segmented; there has been little co-ordination of different investments or

awareness of the interlinkages involved.   The specificity of the
women's situation and of women's problems have certainly not been
adequately dealt with in this regard.

Female labour is all too frequently analysed using a framework
that divides the world into "production" and "reproduction" activities.   The lives of the women who are working in the Sri Lankan
plantation economy suggests that such distinctions must be treated
with care.   "Production" (or "productive activities") is generally
associated with wage labour, while "reproduction" (or "reproductive
activities") is relegated to the twilight world of cultural or even
of "natural" functions.   In more extreme cases this is carried one
step further, with the first being seen as "work" and the second as
"natural aspects of a woman's existence".   This study will try to
show some of the weaknesses of these distinctions, and the importance of understanding the interrelations between these different
activities when discussing the situation and needs of plantation
women.

The methodology employed in this study warrants some explanation and was briefly as follows.   Work on the contemporary situation was carried out in two parts, the first in Colombo and the
second in the field.   In Colombo discussions were held with
officials of the two state plantation bodies, the Janatha Estates
Development Board (JEDB) and the Sri Lankan State Plantations Corporation (SLSPC) and with members of the Ceylon Workers' Congress
(CWC) whose trade union membership is said to comprise some 80 per cent
of the plantation workers.

Based on these discussions and on an analysis of the macro-
data which they provided, it was decided to focus the study on the
JEDB plantations and to establish a representative sample of the
estates that were to be visited.   The main criteria in the decision
to concentrate on one organisation were: (1) the fact that there
appeared to be no discernible difference in the major policy lines
or management practices of the JEDB and the SLSPC; (2) the fact
that the majority of the coconut estates taken over under the Land
Reform Acts were placed under the responsibility of the JEDB when
the Board was created; and (3) the fact that organising fieldwork
with one organisation greatly facilitated the necessary arrangements

and avoided problems when adjustments had to be made.   Doing so
created no apparent distortion.

The sample of estates that were eventually selected for the
present study was drawn up in close consultation with officials of
the JEDB Head Office in Colombo and with the Chairmen and Directors
of the Regional Boards.   The criteria used in making this selection
were fivefold.   It had to include:

1.   low-, medium- and high-grown tea estates;

2.   tea, rubber and coconut estates;

3.   some estates which were good and some which were bad in terms
     of their profitability and their management record in each of
     these categories;

4.   estates nationalised under the 1972 Land Reform Act and the 1975
     Act, with a cross-section of the different organisational forms
     which were introduced;   and

5.   estates under all four Regional Boards in order to take adequate
     account of the geographic and ecological variation that occurred
     from one part of the country to another.

Based on these criteria a travel schedule was drawn up for the
three months during which field interviewing was to take place.
At each of the Regional Boards basic data was collected on all the
estates under its jurisdiction, and after analysis and discussions
on the basis of this data the final selection of estates to be
visited was made.   Fifty-five estates were visited in all.

The interviewing that was carried out on these estates can be
said to have been comprised of two main parts.   The first aimed to
establish an understanding of the industry and of how it operated,
of production, management practices, labour organisation and investment problems for each of the crops, and to provide an overview of
labour conditions.   The second involved direct interviews with
estate workers regarding their situation as they saw it.

Information on the first of these dimensions was obtained from
discussions with the Estate Superintendent and Head Clerk, and with
the Crèche Attendants, Estate Medical Assistants and Welfare Officers
where these existed.   Annual estimates, final accounts, checkrolls

and holiday paybooks were also consulted in order to obtain more
precise statistics and to check various trends that were considered
important.

Interviews with the estate women were carried out both individually and in groups, and they were conducted in a room with no
member of the management and with no men present. Some 352 women
were interviewed under these conditions using a standardised
question format, but employing an open conversation rather than a
normal questionnaire style. Each interview took approximately one-
and-a-half hours, and the women were released from work on pay for
this period. Care was taken to ensure that resident and non-
resident labour were adequately represented within these groups in
accordance with their relative importance on the estates concerned.
Finally, a number of male workers were also interviewed to assess
their opinions on the same issues (this was taken as 10 per cent of
the female sample).

The information that was thus obtained was further checked
from two sources which have been used as supplementary material.
On incomes and on the number of days worked by men and women,
detailed data was collected for a complete division of one estate
(Labookellie, Nuwara Eliya). An in-depth study was also carried
out into the patterns of differentiation amongst workers' families
on one estate (Spring Valley, Badulla). Based on information contained in the estate payroll, three sets of families were selected,
one relatively poor, one average and one relatively rich, and 15
families were selected in all. The representativeness of this
choice was discussed with the management and with the field super-
visors, and the family members were then interviewed in greater
depth with regard to their sources of income, their expenditure
patterns and their indebtedness.

It is in this perspective and on the basis of this information
that the contemporary part of the following study was eventually
written.

TABLE OF CONTENTS

Chapter 1

THE INTERNATIONAL BACKGROUND TO WOMEN IN THE SRI LANKAN PLANTATION SYSTEM

Although the development of Sri Lankan plantations really
began in the 1830s and 1840s, the history of this form of agricultural production and the involvement of female labour within it
goes back much further, even as far back as the fifteenth century.
Women played a significant role in early slave plantations, culti-
vating sugar-cane and later cotton, tobacco and coffee in Latin
America and the Caribbean and in the southern States of the United
States. Women's labour was important for the functioning of these
estates as the latter strove to find their way after the abolition
of slavery, and in time in the expanding large-scale cultivation of
other crops on a plantation basis in Asia, Africa and the Americas.

To be fully understood, the Sri Lankan situation has to be
seen in the light of this much longer and broader historical
experience, which has contributed much to the formation and organisation of these contemporary plantations, and to the particular way in
which female labour was incorporated into this form of production.
In this sense, earlier British plantations in the "New World" can
be seen as immediate forebearers of the Asian case. The development
and consolidation of particular forms and practices of labour control
and labour management in the Caribbean were carried over to British
estates in Sri Lanka by the common colonial Power. Earlier British
experience shaped their thinking, just as this in turn was influenced
by plantations established earlier still. The result was an important line of continuity running throughout the historical development
of this form of production.

This chapter will try to trace the origins and characteristics
of plantation production in order to highlight the emerging patterns
of labour control. It will be argued that these structural features,
and the role of women within them, are important in understanding
women's situation in Sri Lanka today.

The historical background

The origin and early development of plantation agriculture was closely connected to the use of slavery in the cultivation of sugar-cane in the Canary Islands for European markets. This was initiated by the Portuguese, but the lucrativeness of this form of production was soon so apparent that it was adopted by the Spanish, British, French and Dutch settlers in their colonies in the Caribbean and in Latin America. From there plantation production spread to other parts of the tropical and subtropical world.

The historical periods that can be identified in this pattern of diffusion are important in understanding the logic of plantation production at a given point in time. It was influenced by the nature of the European State which governed the colony, and by the way in which it catered to the interests of its dominant groups. Portugal, for example (and later Spain) incorporated feudal elements into its colonisation, reflecting the nature of the Portuguese (and Spanish) State, whereas the British plantations developed in a period in which mercantilist power in Britian was giving way to an industrial bourgeoisie. Under the influence of this bourgeoisie, plantations lost their earlier role of catering to mercantilist or feudal concerns and came to be seen and organised as "capitalist enterprises" functioning to meet the requirement of profitability. The forms of production that were adopted from the Portuguese began to assume a different meaning in the British context, and the way they were incorporated into its colonial economy reflected the needs of a changing economic situation.

The unit and ideology of plantation production

One of the most important prerequisites for plantation production was the existence of an adequate supply of labour. And yet, all of the colonies were characterised by a labour shortage. The Portuguese, the first to tackle this problem, turned to African slaves to solve their dilemma, and with the paucity and destruction of native Indians in the Caribbean the Spanish in time resorted to the same solution. As plantation production spread, so in turn did

the utilisation of slaves to compensate for the inadequate labour
supply.

The way these slaves were incorporated into the plantation
system was influenced to a considerable extent by the background
and earlier experience of settlers, by the system of organisation
they were familiar with, and by that which prevailed "back home" in
their European States.   Even so, there was a strong element of continuity which can be traced in the plantation structure of the
present day.   In the fifteenth century the main unit of organisation in Portuguese society was the extended household.   Slavery, a
Roman legacy to the Iberian peninsula, was kept alive by a trade in
slaves from the seventh century, slaves becoming an integral part of
the household unit.[1]   The latter was essentially a hierarchical
structure, headed by a patriarch and composed of his wife, children,
sons and daughters-in-law, grandchildren, other relatives, unrelated
dependants and also slaves.   The patriarch had absolute authority
within this unit.   The slave was totally dependent upon him and was
integrated into the wider society through his or her position within
this ongoing "household" unit.[2]

This basic structure was retained more or less as it was in
the plantations of the Canary Islands, and the common cultural heri-
tage of the Iberian Peninsula meant that a very similar pattern was
adopted on Spanish plantations in the Caribbean, and Portuguese
Brazil.   The planter was to be seen as a patriarch, his authority
absolute not only over his extended family but also over his slaves.
It was not uncommon for him to have sexual relations with female
slaves, and it was accepted that this "right" extended to the other
male members of his family.   The position of women slaves within
this unit was a particularly lowly one.   At the same time, given
the nature of the influence and control, these early plantations
were essentially feudal production units.[3]

The hierarchical nature of these living and production arrangements was also in itself significant.   The large numbers of African
slaves who were the bulk of the labour force were generally allotted
separate slave huts,[4] while the planter's family lived in the manor
house.   These were the people who were the lowest and highest on
the estate.   Below the planter, in order of rank, came first the

specialists (the ironsmiths, coopers, carpenters, etc.) who were often of mixed blood or were "free"; then came the house slaves (barbers, tailors, seamstresses, cooks); and at the bottom came the bulk of the population, those who worked on the fields and had little to say in any decision affecting their lives. The latter comprised both male and female slaves, people who were mainly of African origin and provided the labour required for day-to-day field operations.

There was a need to rationalise large-scale slavery and female subordination as an integral part of this system. Racialism and sexism grew in significance and became important means of labour control: White signified "skilled" and Black meant "unskilled", and women in this particular form of colonial shorthand were almost invariably seen as inferior to men.[5] These notions were expressed in the authority of the "White" planter over "Black" slaves, and of all men over the slave women, especially Black women (with the "Coloured" mestizos somewhere in between).

The attitude and the relations of production worked out on plantations were then extended to institutions of the larger society because the planters had power. To all intents and purposes they were the Government; they were in a position of authority and control in the larger social order and they applied to it the attitudes and values to which they had become accustomed. This was facilitated by the support of the European State and of the Church, both of which supplemented and reinforced the hold which plantation owners had over the system.

In short, the organisational form that emerged within these plantations was one which was strongly hierarchical and patriarchical in nature. It was rooted in a considerable degree of centralised control and in the value and norms of the semi-feudal Portuguese State. This provided an effective basis for labour control, and for the control of women. Women of the upper classes were "privatised" (contained in the patriarch's household); slave women were invariably considered inferior and subjected to male control at every level. The basic structural characteristics of this organisational form were carried on into the British period, with the same hierarchical form and division of labour because of the efficiency of these labour relations in meeting the needs of the market economy.

Slavery and capitalism on British plantations

At the same time, for all this continuity, the experience of British plantations gave rise to certain adaptations in the production unit. Firmly based as far as form was concerned on the Portuguese legacy, it was sustained by a very different ideology, reflecting needs and demands of capitalism in Britain. The "yeoman farmers" who were the basic unit of society in Cromwellian Britain had a tradition with no place for slaves in it. Nevertheless, it was these farmers who moved to the Caribbean and who eventually found that the cultivation of sugar-cane needed labour; slavery was a readily available option and they had to come to terms with the idea of using the cheap and plentiful supply of African slaves.

This plantation that emerged was based on the concept of the "firm", with slaves "assumed to be part of the capital equipment". Heavily influenced by the industrial organisation that was growing in England, the "company" was to prove instrumental in bringing scattered groups of "yeomen" holdings under centralised control which at the same time used imported slave labour. As such it could attract credit from foreign stockholders and could introduce new capital equipment and other innovations, and generally increase the profitability of cultivation. At the same time this newly emerging form of plantation production remained firmly based in the "non-capitalist" labour relations and earlier forms of labour organisation as an effective means of labour control.

It was these developments taking place in the Caribbean that set the stage for future plantation development in Asia and elsewhere in the nineteenth century. In short, three factors were particularly important: the first was the emergence of a laissez-faire economy with its emphasis on private investment and profit; second was the incorporation of "quasi-feudal" relations into a capitalist production system; and third was the retention of the old patriarchal and hierarchical organisation and of an ideology demanding strict respect for those who were in power. The implications of these will emerge in the course of this study.

Women in the British plantations

This shift in the "capitalisation" of plantation production
had significant implications for female labour. Firstly, all
labour and especially female labour was now evaluated in terms of
the need to increase the "profitability" of the "capitalist enterprise". Innovations for increasing "efficiency" were encouraged
and jobs which involved working with these new machines took on a
"higher status". These were dominated by the male workers while
women were concentrated in the labour-intensive, time-consuming
tasks. Secondly, women's roles as fieldworkers and in the reproduction of the labour force was viewed in terms of efficiency and of
benefits in relation to costs. Thirdly, with the increasing costs
of the slave trade and the imminent threat of slave emancipation,
there was encouragement of marriages and "nuclear" household units
among the slaves.

As long as the slave trade was cheap, slave labour (whether it
was men or women) was now seen primarily as a "cheap input" into
estate production regardless of the arduousness involved or the pain
endured. Female slaves were "part and parcel" of the means of production, and they were worked as hard as any male slaves.[6] However,
even if they were numerically less important, they were more
exploited. In many cases, they were the majority of field workers
under male supervision of one sort or the other, engaged in tasks
which even today are considered amongst the hardest on sugar plantations. Further, they were subjected to sexual abuse from men at
all levels.[7] In short, the life and tasks of female slaves
reflected the following characteristics: a concentration in activities that entailed very little capital equipment; which were time-
consuming; had a low status; were essential to the running of the
plantation; were subjected to male supervision and authority, which
was often expressed in physical abuse and sexual violation.

Changing attitudes towards work and the family

With the increasing costs of the slave trade there was a concerted effort to promote and encourage the reproduction of slaves
on existing plantations.[8] Measures were introduced to encourage

the formation of nuclear families, and this in turn served to cate-
gorise a certain range of activities as falling within the household domain.   These were now seen as "private" or "personal" activities (separate from the rest of the "economy" and "production").

In the concrete Caribbean situation, these notions meant adjust-
ment in the "loose" life to which slave women had become accustomed.
Most had experienced sexual relationships with several men; children
were viewed primarily in relation to women and rarely associated
with a particular father; and caring for them was seen as largely
her responsibility.   Women emerged "in charge" of these household
affairs (although the men were ideologically seen as "head" of the
unit) while both provided labour for the estates.[9]   As far as the
planters were concerned this often "economic" arrangement provided
them with the labour they required while freeing them of the concern
for and the expense of reproduction activities that were now carried
out within the confines of the household unit.   Catering now to
these needs and services, women tended to be seen as the "private"
property of men while the "private" unit now provided an unseen subsidy paid by women to the wages paid on the estates.

In a wider sense, the sexual division of labour and the male-
dominated ideology sustaining it was tied up with the structure of
the production system, because those controlling plantations were
generally controlling society.   Sex exploitation was institutionally
engrained and it existed at every level.   The values that were
attached to particular tasks were not only ranked in a hierarchical
order but they were expected to satisfy, justify and to perpetuate
an existing situation in which large numbers of workers could be
exploited as efficiently as possible.   Women because of their sex
and because of their inferior "rank" were exploited more.

The abolition of slavery, and the consequent depletion of the
slave labour force on the various plantations, forced the management
to look to alternative sources of labour supply and to introduce
different kinds of labour systems with which to incorporate this
labour into plantation production.   The responses which gradually
emerged were naturally varied, reflecting the many differences in
local conditions, the background and experience of the people
involved and the nature of the crop.   Although seasonal labour was

one source of cheap manpower there were "uncertainties" with this
and the British colonies found a valuable alternative in indentured
labour.

Indentured labour involved the importation of people from
another country or another region, bonded specifically for work on
estates and bound by strict rules and contracts to ensure that they
abided by these arrangements.   This system was introduced in the
Guyanas and the British West Indies, and although various indentured
immigrants were brought across (including Chinese and Portuguese) it
was the East Indians who were to constitute the main and most successful source of immigrant labour.[10]   This "new form of slavery" was
opposed in a great many quarters, but still came to provide the most
important alternative to slavery on British plantations.[11]

The Sri Lankan plantation economy started developing in this
climate of change from slavery to other forms of labour control.
In this situation labour was still very much viewed as a means of
production.   It had to be acquired for any investment in plantation
production, and this supply (once it was there) had to be channelled
and controlled in such a way as to promote efficiency and profitability for those who invested.   Past experience in plantation
cultivation provided a wealth of possibilities in this respect as
well as insights into problems associated with this form of production.   The labour system and the structure of the Sri Lankan plantations reflect this concern and this continuity.   More important in
the context of this analysis, they carried over a particular attitude
towards women and towards women's labour which was concretised in a
particularly disadvantageous manner in the plantations of Sri Lanka.

Notes

[1] J.A. Saco: Historia de la esclavitud de la raza africana en
el nuevo mundo (Barcelona, 1879), Vol. 1, pp. 35-36.

[2] S.M. Greenfield: "Slavery and the plantation in the New
World" in Journal of Inter-American Studies (Gainsville, University
of Miami), Jan. 1969, Vol. II, No. 1.

[3] Independent Iberian capitalism was hampered by the fact that
it was subservient to that developing in northern Italy, and it
served primarily as a channel through which colonial riches flowed

to other rising capitalist nations (the United Kingdom, the
Netherlands and Italy).   Furthermore, the riches that remained in
Portugal and Spain were "as a rule, not realised capitalistically
but became feudal hoarding" (M. Kossak: "Common aspects and distinctive features in colonial Latin America" in Science and Society
(New York, John Jay College), Spring 1973, Vol. XXXVII, No. 1,
pp. 14-15.

4 They were initially segregated according to sex, but later
allowed to form nuclear family units.   The significance of these
aspects will be discussed later.

5 M. Cranton: Searching for the invisible man: Slaves and
plantation life in Jamaica (London, 1978) Table 46, p. 180.

6 O. Patterson: The sociology of slavery: an analysis of the
origins, development and structure of Negro slave society in Jamaica
(London, Reading and Fakenham, MacGibbon and Kee, 1967), p. 105.

7 Cranton, op. cit., 1978, p. 146, Figure 28.   Here we
observe that women were consistently more than 50 per cent of the
field force.   The sexual exploitation of female slaves has been
widely described (Patterson, op. cit., 1967, p. 42).

8 For details of this concern and of measures taken by the
French, British and Spanish Crowns in this matter see M. d'Auberteuil:
Considerations sur l'état present de la colonie française de
St. Dominique (Paris, 1776-77), Vol. 2, p. 62; Patterson, op. cit.,
1967, pp. 105-106; and G.M. Hall: Social control in slave plantation societies (Baltimore and London, Johns Hopkins University Press,
1971).

9 R.T. Smith: "Family structure and plantation system in the
New World", in Plantation systems of the New World (Washington D.C.,
Pan American Union and Research Institute for the Study of Man,
1959).

10 J.A. Weller: The East Indian indenture in Trinidad (Rio
Piedras, Institute of Caribbean Studies, University of Puerto Rico,
1968); see also C. Thomas: "Agrarian change in a plantation
economy: the case of Guyana", in D. Ghai, A. Khan, E. Lee and
S. Radwan (eds.): Agrarian systems and rural development (London,
the Macmillan Press Ltd., 1979).   For examples of indentured labour
from other countries see J. Paige: Agrarian revolution - social
movements and export agriculture in the underdeveloped world (New
York, Free Press, 1975), p. 143; and C.D. Scott: Machetes,
machines and agrarian reform: the political economy of technical
choice in the Peruvian sugar industry, 1954-74 (Norwich, School of
Development Studies, University of East Anglia, 1979), p. 78 and
A.H. Adamson: Sugar without slaves: the political economy of
British Guyana 1838-1904 (New Haven and London, Yale University
Press, 1978).

11 See the despatch of 15 Feb. 1840 of Lord John Russell where
he refuses to take responsibility for a process which "may lead to
a dead loss of life on the one hand, or on the other to a new system
of slavery" (quoted in Adamson, op. cit., 1972).

Chapter 2

THE EMERGENCE AND STRUCTURE OF THE
SRI LANKAN PLANTATION SECTOR

Earlier experience in other countries with plantation production
had a considerable influence on the pattern that was in time to
emerge in Sri Lanka.   The form that Sri Lankan plantations took,
the organisation of labour and the types of management practices
that they assumed reflected an amalgam of past and present.   The
British colonial policy of _laissez-faire_, in which their Caribbean
estates evolved and prospered, provided the backcloth to British
investments in Sri Lanka just as in other parts of the tropical world.
British capital seeking new and alternative sources of profitable
investment brought with it a body of accumulated experience with
large-scale production from other colonies, and certain ideas as to
what was viable and what was not.

At the same time Sri Lanka had its own history and its own social
structure, and one which was in many ways quite distinctive from
that which the British had encountered in the Caribbean.   Sri Lankan
plantations were bound to have their peculiarities, while maintain-
ing continuity with the past.   And this was essentially what was
to happen.   Sri Lanka was to become a "plantation economy" based
on the use of indentured labour, similar to that employed in Guyana,
Mauritius, Trinidad and even Jamaica, promoted by the British colonial apparatus in order to further the interests of its own investors.
It was to inherit a form of plantation organisation which was not
only hierarchical, but also patriarchal in nature.   It was to place
considerable weight on respect for authority, and to reflect a particular blend of features from earlier systems heavily influenced
by local conditions, and in no way more so than in patterns of labour
organisation and labour control.

The particular form which the present plantations take in Sri
Lanka can only be understood fully in this perspective, as indeed
can attitudes to women plantation workers, the utilisation of female
labour, the tasks which are allotted only to women and the economic
and social discrimination to which they are subjected.   This chapter
sets out to trace the development of the Sri Lankan plantation system in the light of the past, to trace its internal differentiation
and the forces to which it has been subjected and has responded
over time, and it does so in order to set the stage for later discussion of the role of women in contemporary plantations.

This chapter itself is structered in five main parts arranged chronologically and dealing with (1) coffee and the Sri Lankan plantation model; (2) the development of alternative crops in the nineteenth century; (3) the plantation sector in the period from 1900 until independence in 1948; (4) post-independence prior to nationalisation; and (5) the plantation sector from nationalisation to the present day.

Coffee and the Sri Lankan plantation model

The most significant developments in the Sri Lankan plantations began in the nineteenth century under British rule and they were centred around the cultivation of coffee, tea, rubber and coconuts.[1] Since that time they have dominated the economic development of the island, and they have been a persistent and major focus in political debate. Planters dictated economic policy in much of the colonial period, the plantation sector provided the basis of capitalist expansion in the island, and even today it is the largest single foreign exchange earner and the largest contributor to the country's gross national product, as well as being its largest single employer.

Although coffee was introduced to Sri Lanka in the eighteenth century, it was mainly grown by indigenous smallholders until the late 1830s.[2] By this time, the international situation was such that there was greater demand and a more lucrative climate for its cultivation.[3] The abolition of the slave trade and the equalisation of import duties on Ceylonese and West Indian coffee in Britain meant higher relative prices for Ceylonese coffee on the London market.[4]

In 1833 a series of government reforms were introduced in Sri Lanka (the Colebrook-Cameron Reforms), formalising the adoption of a laissez-faire policy on the island itself, and together the changed market situation and the development of this new ideology created a favourable situation for the investment into and expansion of plantation production. The colonial Government made the sale of lands to those who wanted to grow the crop very much easier.[5] By the late 1830s the trend was firmly established, and following a certain amount of experimentation, coffee estates began to spread rapidly in the Central Highlands.[6] Speculators also bought land directly from villagers, although most of the early expansion took place at

higher elevations on land purchased from the Crown at public auctions.
Between 1844 and 1860, 105,486 acres were alienated to European
investors in this way.[7]

The following sections will examine the pattern of production
that emerged within this context with particular emphasis upon two
dimensions: labour supply and the pattern of recruitment on the
one hand, and the organisation of the unit of production on the other.

Labour supply and the pattern of recruitment

As we have seen, one of the essential requirements for plantation agriculture was the existence of an adequate, and adequately
disciplined, labour force. Some labour was required for coffee
production throughout the year, and different tasks such as the
preparation of the land, nurturing the crop and its harvesting had
to be undertaken and had to be completed within a definite and rather
limited period of time. However, the demand for labour was not
constant but in part at least seasonal, with a peak demand during
the harvest period - in this case normally from August to November.

Labour of this kind (and particularly permanent labour) was not
forthcoming from the Sinhalese population. These were people who
had their own land in the village, in comparison with which the plantation demanded "unending, monotonous, day-to-day work ... which
left little or no opportunity for the workers to carry on separate
occupations in their homes".[8]

The absence of a large landless proletariat to provide the
labour that was needed for these plantations led the British planters
to look elsewhere, and experience had shown that a valuable alternative was indentured labour. This they found in the famine-prone
districts in southern India which had a large number of low caste
(or outcaste) landless agricultural workers whose economic and
social situation was very severe.[9] The planters found that if these
workers were offered higher wages, they could be induced to accept
the work the Sinhalese rejected,[10] and from 1839 there was large-
scale emigration from these areas to Sri Lankan plantations.[11]

This low caste and outcaste labour was recruited and imported
to Sri Lanka under what has since come to be known as the "Kangany
system". The kangany was a man from one of the higher subcastes
of the Sudra caste who was employed by the planters as a recruiter.
He had originated from these Indian villages, and he offered induce-
ments to kinsmen and other people to come to Sri Lanka in order to

undertake work on a particular plantation. Those who went received
a cash advance to meet their expenses during the journey. The
labour force thus formed was subdivided into a number of smaller
groups, each under a sub or silara kangany.[12] Recruitment involved
a difficult sea voyage and a lengthy march through the interior of
the island. The entire journey was fraught with difficulties; few
or no health facilities were provided, and large numbers of those
that set out to seek their "fortunes" failed in fact to survive the
hazardous journey.[13]

The unit of production and organisation of labour

The plantations ranged from 20-1,000 acres. Between 1833 and
1860 the average size was about 100 acres[14], most being individually owned or held in partnership.[15] The estates followed the
pattern developed by the British elsewhere, particularly in the
Caribbean; they were organised on strict hierarchical lines,
patriarchal in structure, with complete obedience and respect
required from the labour force. The head kangany was the direct
controler of labour and this control was maintained in no small
measure by the fact that he came from a higher caste.

The superintendent or the Periya Dorai was the organisational
head responsible for plantation efficiency and management. He was
usually a European aided by (usually European) assistants. Under
them came the office staff (accountants, etc.), who were Tamils
with some western education (but not associated with Tamil workers).
Below them came the head kangany, the sub (or silara) kanganies,
and the workers themselves.

The head kangany was the key figure in the organisation and
control of the labour force.[16] The management paid him for every
worker he brought to Sri Lanka, and he was acknowledged to be their
de facto head. He supervised and transacted the estate's financial
affairs vis-à-vis "coolies", even if not actually paying their wages.
He was often the sole debtor to the estate; all advances were made
through him, passed on via the subkanganies working on a day-to day
basis on individual debts. For the estate management this was
convenient because they were able to deal with one man, but it also
gave the kangany a great deal of power - especially when he assisted
the estate in financing its workers.[17] This strengthened his
bargaining position vis-à-vis management and gave him enormous
leverage over his men.

This system was in turn reinforced by a series of practices, one of the most important of which was the tundu system. The tundu was a written statement prepared by an employer indicating the amount of money that a particular worker owed the estate and which, once paid, enabled the worker to seek employment on an estate elsewhere.[18] However, since all financial transactions were made through the head kangany, he was in a position to arrange with another superintendent to "buy off" these debts, in this way shifting his gang of "coolies" from estate to estate, depending on which offered him the greatest rewards. In a situation of labour shortage, this was often lucrative for the kangany, and since on this point the superintendent was very vulnerable, it was also an effective means of increasing the kangany's power.[19]

In addition to this function as the recognised head of the labour under him, the kangany also supervised work in the fields. For this task he was paid "head money", a sum for each worker who actually turned out. In this way the kangany (and through him the subkanganies) played a crucial role in ensuring a high turnout and in organising the daily labour force, a task for which he had in turn to be reimbursed. He also received a fixed salary for other "special duties".[20]

The kangany also controlled the labour force under him in other ways. In most cases it was the kangany, for example, who ran the estate shop. There "the workers were the victims of all the evils of the 'truck system', including high prices and indebtedness to the shopkeeper who provided loans at high rates of interest".[21] The method by which workers were paid in the early years was such that one month's wage was paid to the worker and the next to the kangany to be offset against the worker's debt; it was "a system which increased the opportunities for the swindling of illiterate workers".[22] Finally, the kangany was responsible for the welfare of the workers under him; he represented them in the settlement of labour disputes, he settled disputes between individual workers and was often called upon to adjudicate in family quarrels. All these factors served to make the head kangany almost a "patriarch", a wealthy, influential and powerful figure in the running of estates, and an important force to strengthen semi-feudal and patriarchical attitudes within the system.

The subkangany usually worked on the fields as a worker or as an overseer. For this he received a "name", entitling him to a day's pay, and "pence money", a sum for each worker of his gang who turned out for work. His dealings with the management were generally through the head kangany, though in some cases, he also owed money directly to the estate. He was the sole creditor to the individual workers who composed his gang. Each subkangany group (for the labour was in practice organised on such a basis) was relatively homogenous in terms of caste, and was often composed of people related to one another.[23] The subkangany supervised the financial affairs of his particular gang.

The worker was at the bottom of the whole hierarchical order. In the first two decades of plantation enterprise his daily wages ranged from 4d. to 9d. per working day of 10 to 11 hours, and it had risen to about 10d. per day in the 1860s.[24] This, as we have seen, was paid to the worker once in two months; most estates supplied imported Indian rice to their workers, the cost of which was deducted from their wage. In return, these people worked on the coffee estate, they were given free accommodation in a room shared with some ten or so other people in a barrack line, and in most cases they suffered an extremely hard and severely disciplined existence.

The ability of the worker to choose his place of work was also severely restricted by other factors once he had agreed to work on a particular plantation. As immigrant labour became more and more important for coffee estates, the need for a stable labour force became significant and the State began to pass laws and regulations to govern relations between employers and employees. The most prominent of these were the Master-Servant Laws (under Ordinance No. 5 of 1841) which introduced labour contracts for up to one, and later (under Ordinance No. 11 of 1865) for up to three years.[25]

The implication of this legislation for the individual worker was that he had to satisfy his contract and pay his debts before he was in a position to leave an estate. Thus while the Ordinances "made ample provision for the protection of the immigrant worker ... the coolie unaware of its existence, ignorant of his own rights, or apprehensive of still further annoyance, failed in almost any one instance to appeal to them for protection or to call on the local magistrate for assistance. His disposition and habit was to suffer

in silence".[26] The cost of his travel from India to Sri Lanka had
to be repaid; he invariably started his life on the estate with a
debt,[27] and this was exacerbated by the system of payment as a
result of which he received no wage until he had worked on the estate
for a full two months.   No doubt this facilitated labour management,
but it placed the worker in victimised circumstances.

In addition to all these direct constraints, the worker was
also confronted within the estate by a strong caste system which
influenced his relationship with his co-workers.   The kangany system
fostered the maintenance of traditional norms and prejudices, and
this was reflected in and strengthened by the general practice of
allocating line rooms according to caste.   In fact, segregation
and the provision of "acceptable arrangements" in the layout of
buildings were of importance; they were taken into account when
the lines were being constructed, and the weight that was attached
to such arrangements highlighted the significance of caste in the
life of the workers.[28]

Summary: Coffee and the Sri Lankan plantation model

To summarise, the estates operated in a very favoured situation.
The planters were influential in colonial society, and they were
able to secure privileged treatment from the State.   The system of
land sales worked very much in their interests,[29] they were exempt
from land tax,[30] they were given priority in infrastructural investment,[31] given assistance in the recruitment of Indian labour,[32] and
allowed to import Indian rice to feed these workers.[33] Laws were
enacted to meet their own interests; the Master and Servant Laws
served to secure their labour force and their lands were protected
from encroachment and damage by Sinhalese villagers.[34] The system
served to promote the interests of the coffee planter.   What is
more, while in principle the plantation system worked with wage
labour, it was by no means "free".

Alternative crops and the spread of plantation agriculture

Coffee production on plantations, once it had started, responded
favourably to international demand and the lucrative prices that
were being offered.   But for a short period between 1846 and 1850
(when the island felt the negative effect of the world depression),
"king coffee reigned supreme", and did so until the end of the 1860s.[35]

Production expanded, prices rose or at worst remained stable at
favourable levels, and the volume of produce exported rose quite
dramatically.[36] Profits increased, the need for higher levels of
investment became apparent and, in response to this, sterling companies began to be formed in Britain and agency houses began to play
a more significant role in the financing and management of individual
estates.[37]

The collapse of coffee and development of tea

Coffee cultivation in Sri Lanka was to have a short history.
A coffee leaf fungus, Hemileia Vastatrix, made its appearance in 1869
and it soon spread widely.   A rise in prices resulted in further
expansion in the 1870s, but it was achieved at the expense of a fall
in the yield per acre.   By 1881, the decline was rapid and comprehensive, and by 1886 the Sri Lankan coffee industry was, "for all
practical purposes, dead".[38]   Tea replaced coffee and became the
most important plantation crop.

Only a few of the coffee planters were in a position to take
up tea cultivation on their estates; the majority, and especially
those with smaller holdings, were incapable of doing so and were
completely ruined.[39]

Rubber and changing labour requirements

Rubber was introduced to Sri Lanka in 1876, but production was
not carried out on a significant scale before the twentieth century.
The exorbitant price it commanded in international markets, in the
wake of the rapidly expanding automobile industry, made rubber cultivation an attractive and profitable proposition.[40]   Continuing stagnation in the price of tea and the lower level of capital required in
rubber production, were together sufficient to stimulate a shift to
its cultivation.[41]   From 1900 to 1907, the acreage under rubber
increased from 1,750 acres to 150,000 acres.[42]   It was soon a significant contributor to the country's export earnings, and by 1913
its foreign exchange earnings were three quarters of those from tea.[43]

Unlike tea, however, rubber cultivation was attractive to a number of Sri Lankans.   As the good rubber land was concentrated in mid
and low country areas and thereby comparatively close to the Sinhalese
villages, and as there was little to be gained by way of economies
of scale, an important part of total rubber production came from
peasant smallholdings.[44]

The shift from coffee to tea and later to rubber also had repercussions on the structure and growth of the labour force. These stemmed mainly from the different labour requirements of these crops, and the poverty of Sinhalese villagers, but they were also influenced by the growth and development of the plantation sector. Unlike coffee, which needed extra labour at certain peak seasons, tea plucking and rubber tapping had to be carried on throughout the year. This in turn created a demand for a more regular and more stable labour force, with relatively little seasonal fluctuation. Furthermore, the rapid expansion of tea and rubber production generated pressures towards an over-all increase in the labour force.

This new situation had three important effects on the pattern of immigration. Firstly, there was a shift towards longer periods of stay in the island and longer contracts, often up to three years.[45] Secondly, the age and sex composition of immigrants underwent change as people began to migrate with wives and children, rather than on an individual basis.[46] Thirdly, the over-all number of immigrants increased and the net increase in the Indian labour force was quite substantial.[47]

As far as the plantations were concerned, the most crucial change was related to the growing importance of female labour.[48] This was the direct result of the new immigration pattern, the patriarchal form and environment of the estates enabling the planters to employ female labour at a low wage rate. The history, logic and economics of the estate system favoured the concentration of women in the time-consuming tasks with long hours of work and lower rates of pay than those offered to men (discussed in Chapter 1, p. 7). Tea plucking and rubber tapping, jobs which were the most labour intensive and which had to be done all times of the year, became principal areas of female specialisation.

Coconuts and Sinhalese involvement

The other important plantation crop was the coconut. This was primarily a peasant crop and it had a much longer history than the others.[49]

Coconut plantations differed from tea and rubber in several respects, in terms of their labour and capital requirements, their ownership patterns and their role in the over-all development of the national economy. These factors had important implications for the political future and labour organisation of the sector, even though it maintained a similar basic structure in terms of its management.

Firstly, the labour required was considerably less than in the case of either tea or rubber.[50] This was basically because the coconut palm does not need systematic human attention and is likely to produce a fairly stable number of nuts each year for at least 50 years. Most of the labour is needed for harvesting and weeding and the remaining tasks (application of fertiliser, ploughing the soil and moisture conservation, the burying of husks, control of pests, etc.) can be spread throughout the rest of the year, depending on particular climatic conditions. The initial clearing was carried out by leasing the land out on ande (sharecropping) for the temporary cultivation of chena and other garden crops.[51]

The result was that plantations used labour from surrounding villages which they were able to employ on a casual basis. The few permanent employees on the larger estates were given living accommodation similar to that provided in the case of rubber and tea. Men were generally employed for harvesting, draining, ploughing and harrowing, while the women were concentrated in weeding, husking operations for mulch and the collection of nuts. Most operations were done with the aid of casual labour.

Secondly, the coconut plantation needed little capital investment for its production. Most of the processing for coconut oil, copra and dessicated coconut was carried out in separately owned mills and only the cultivation and husking was done on the estate. Hardly any machines were necessary at all. Thirdly, coconut plantations were largely locally owned. The principal investors were the low country Sinhalese and to a lesser extent Sri Lankan Tamils. Having accumulated their wealth from arrack renting, graphite mining or trade, they found this a lucrative form of investment.[52] They found that with only a minimal amount of capital it was soon possible to amass considerably more by taking advantage of the rising price of coconuts and coconut products, the majority of the production being sold as "green nuts" for the domestic market.

The twentieth century until independence

The period from 1900 to 1947 was notable on two important scores. Firstly, the production and export of all three plantation crops experienced sharp fluctuations, to a large extent determined by external forces. Secondly, the workers' plight was more widely publicised and for the first time politicisation and trade unionism began to emerge. These two dimensions will be explored in turn.

"The instability of an export economy"

Since the plantation sector was primarily export-oriented, it was significantly affected by the vagaries of the international market.   In this the most striking events were the two world wars and the period of the depression in the 1930s.   Output and growth escalated, only to vary sharply in the face of these crises.   All three crops were substantially affected, although rubber and coconut were to prove more sensitive than tea.   Nevertheless, plantation crops continued to comprise the bulk of the country's export earnings, from the 1920s accounting for over 90 per cent.

By the second decade of the twentieth century, all three crops were already firmly established.   With the First World War came a boom in the rubber industry.   At the same time the Government placed a freeze on the price of tea which negatively affected local production.[53]   Coconut was favourable affected by the rise in prices, and exports of copra and dessicated coconut (in terms of both value and quantity) steadily increased.[54]

In the postwar period the plantation sector expanded, and this momentum was maintained until the depression in the 1930s when all three export crops were badly hit.[55]   Rubber was worst affected, with a massive decline in output, employment and prices.[56]   Coconut prices were less than half of those a decade earlier and exports of copra and dessicated coconut fell.   Tea was in a relatively favoured position, and its export earnings were not substantially reduced.[57]

More important for the labour force on the plantations was the rising tide of unemployment and the fall in income.   With a decline in price and restrictions placed on output, the estate management sought to reduce the wages of workers, and they were lowered three times between 1931 and 1933.[58]   Even so, these successive reductions were not enough to prevent widespread unemployment.   The number of Indian workers fell 23 per cent between 1929 and 1933 while the non-Indian workforce, which was considerably smaller, fell by a little over 17 per cent.[59]   The worst hit were workers on the rubber estates, who were reduced by half.[60]   In every case however, the women workers, with their lower wage rates and their weak and marginalised positions in the estate workforce, suffered the most.   Nor were redundancies restricted to workers;   they affected the staff, most of those who lost their jobs being Sri Lankan.[61]

When war broke out in 1939 over-all export growth had been
resumed, and it continued to increase.   The plantations were not
allowed to take advantage of increases in prices; Britain had
entered into a contract agreement with the island in order to ensure
itself of continuous supplies and the normal "free" market price
system was abolished.[62] By 1942 nearly 97 per cent of Sri Lanka's
exports fell under this scheme and sold well below the prevailing
international prices.[63] The net effect of this was to limit output
and if profitability did not fall it was only maintained at the
expense of labour as import prices rose twice as fast as export
prices.[64]

On the plantations themselves, the overriding concern was with
raising current output; proper maintenance procedures were rarely
observed (especially in the case of rubber and coconut) and this
often meant output at the cost of future growth.[65] In such a situation the labour force was exploited to the maximum.   There was a
fall in real wages on tea and rubber estates in the first three
years of the war although from 1944 to 1945 there was again an
increase.   This can be seen from the table below:

Index of wages of tea and rubber estate workers

Year	Minimum money wage	Cost of living index	Real wages 100: (1)-(2)
	(1)	(2)	(3)
1939	100	100	100
1940	100	107	94
1941	109	109	92
1942	115	154	107
1943	201	196	103
1944	212	211	100
1945	244	222	110

Source: Corea, op. cit., p. 209

As a whole, the period brought out the vulnerability of both
workers and management to fluctuations in the international market.
Production began to be controlled on the basis of international
agreements as the planters felt the need for positive co-ordinated
organisation in order to avoid a repetition of those events.

Politicisation and trade union development

Up to the twentieth century very little had been done for plantation workers.[66] It was only then that nationalist leaders and
the Indian Government began to protest against the more glaring
injustices in the situation of the Indian workforce in Sri Lanka.
The condition of these workers was highlighted by Indian members
in the Legislative Council who pointed to changes that needed to
be brought about.   The most important of these members was Natesa
Aiyar (1926-31) who was subsequently involved in trying to organise
the first trade union amongst plantation workers.

The Education Ordinance of 1920, under which compulsory ele-
mentary vernacular education had to be provided to children on the
estates, resulted in a higher level of literacy and a greater awareness of struggles that were taking place in the rest of the country.
With the circulation of Tamil language newspapers from Tamil-Nadu,
the workers were increasingly in touch with anti-imperialist struggles occurring in India.[67] They were becoming far more aware of
their own situation and of the nature of their relations with the
kangany and the estate management.   Legislations in 1909 and 1921
had done away with the earlier tundu system and had made it possible
for them to break free of the worst and most distressing ties of
indebtedness.[68] Perhaps for the first time, the workers saw the
possibility of bettering their own situation and of joint organisation and struggle to bring this about.

From 1925 onwards, Natesa Aiyar travelled widely in the tea
and rubber areas, attempting to organise workers, urging them to
voice their demands, and writing about the conditions to which
they were subjected.[69] At the same time, as Indian member in the
Legislative Council, he, with his supporters, was vociferous in
championing the cause of the plantation worker.[70] As a result of
this cumulative political pressure and of that being exerted by
the Indian Government, a Minimum Wages Ordinance was passed in 1927,
raising wages which had in many cases been stagnant since the nineteenth century.[71]

One of the most important events in the politicisation of the
workers was the franchise given them under the Donoughmore Commission
Recommendations in 1931.   Nearly 100,000 Indians gained the right
to vote, and suddenly became a focus for politicians vying for
their support.   Political activity and awareness sharpened though
there was little concern with discrimination between men and women.

In the same year Natesa Aiyar attempted to organise a separate
trade union movement for plantation workers, the All-Ceylon Estate
Labour Federation with its head office in the tea-planting district
of Hatton.   Through petitions, mass meetings and publications the
Federation began to voice the grievances of the workers it would
represent, but again the issues it raised were rarely at all specific
to women.

Moreover, this movement was in practice to be very short-lived.
What finally caused its collapse was the depression, and along
with it widespread unemployment and fall in the minimum wage.[72]
The latter was taken up by the Federation; it organised meetings
to rouse public support, but it was not successful.   The threat
of unemployment was far too great.   A.E. Goonesinha, leader of the
Ceylon Labour Union, (the strongest urban based labour movement)
did not support it.[73]   Faced with economic crisis, the Sinhalese
felt their employment threatened by Tamils.   The latter they saw
depriving their people of jobs and in the process trying to dominate
them politically.   Despite encouragement from Indian nationalist
leaders such as Gandhi and Nehru, the trade union movement in the
estate sector had collapsed by 1933.[74]

By the end of the 1930s the trade union movement had begun
to re-emerge under the leadership of the Ceylon Indian Congress,
a combination of several Tamil organisations which had come together
with the help of Nehru in 1939.[75]   The Lanka Samaja Party, the
first "left" party in Sri Lanka, also began to organise workers
on estates to form trade unions.   As a result, the number of strikes
on estates began to increase and "by 1940 almost every estate was
affected by unionism, strikes and labour unrest".[76]   Strikes were
far less prevalent during the war with a collective agreement in
force but after that they again increased.   From 1946 the estates
were consistently the largest section of the country's labour force
to go on strike.[77]   The reasons for the strikes ranged from discontent with methods of labour management to nation-wide protests
against government efforts to introduce legislation.[78]   But rarely
again did the situation of women - the wage differentials, longer
hours of work or their available facilities - emerge as a serious
theme in their various demands.

To sum up, this period witnessed the beginnings of trade union
movements among plantation labour.   In the course of this the
base and potential grew as workers became more aware of their own

situation, and as they began to protest. However, on the whole
they were isolated from the trade union movement in the rest of
the country.

It is significant to note that while, according to interviews,
women did participate in trade union affairs during this period,
little mention has since been made of them in analyses of these
movements. There has been a widespread tendency (however implicit)
to view the trade union movement as a male domain, a feature no
doubt reinforced by the women themselves and no doubt derived in
no small part from the patriarchal nature of the estate situation.
Furthermore, there is little evidence to show that they scored any
real success in ameliorating the lot of the women workers.

The estate sector from
independence to nationalisation

The period from 1948 when Sri Lanka won its independence from
Britain to 1972, when the first land reform laws were enacted,
witnessed a shift of government priorities away from the estate
sector, and a considerable loss in its political and economic power.
The most important fact as far as the workers were concerned was
that the new Government passed a series of immigration and citizenship laws which resulted in the disenfranchisement of the majority
of the Indian estate workers.

By 1946 the Indian population on the estates was 665,855, about
10 per cent of the country's population. After independence the
citizenship requirements for Indian residents were revised and laid
out in the Ceylon Citizenship Act of 1948 and the Indian and Pakis-
tani Residents (Citizenship) Act of 1949. The property and wealth
required under the former Act automatically excluded the vast
majority of the plantation workers from citizenship and hence from
political franchise and representation. The 1948 Act laid down
conditions for citizenship by registration. However, the total
number of people who were granted Sri Lankan citizenship under these
acts was as low as 16 per cent of those who applied.[79] The Sirimavo-
Shastri Pact concluded in 1964 between the Governments of Sri Lanka
and India laid down that of the 975,000 workers who were still without citizenship, a certain number (some 525,000 persons) were to
be compulsorily repatriated. The legislation that was necessary

to implement this agreement was passed in June 1967, and those who wanted to apply for Sri Lankan citizenship were asked to do so in 1968. The delays in the repatriation to India (together with the 150,000 "stateless" persons who still remained under this Pact) created a situation in which the plantation sector was serviced by a large "stateless" population with no political rights in the country in which they lived and in which they worked.

The implications of these trends for the labour force were quite significant. Emphasis was increasingly placed on productivity in order to counteract the effects of higher taxation and to offset the disadvantages of lower government priority. To achieve this there were widespread redundancies, and since it was to be achieved by increasing output rather than by heavy replanting or other care, the unemployment affected men much more than women. The average number of hours work offered to male workers per week dropped from 160 to 140 in the 1960s.[80] Apart from the accepted division of labour on the estates, the fact that male labour was more expensive than female labour tended if anything to reinforce this trend.

The production crisis and higher levels of taxation created an atmosphere of uncertainty regarding the reliability of profits within this sector, and capital began to flee in search of more secure or more lucrative forms of investment. From the late 1950s this trend was to strengthen in the face of political debates which constantly raised the spectre of nationalisation. In some cases this led to the physical deterioration of the estates; companies started intensifying production to use up capital and to evade restrictions on capital repatriation by means of increasing profit remittances. Replanting and other cultivation practices began to be neglected and many of the estates were simply operated on a "care and maintenance" basis.

These factors and their implications weakened the estate sector both politically and economically. Its role as the leading sector of the economy was slowly undermined, and it became little more than a source of funds for welfare politics on which the political stability of the nation rested.

From nationalisation to the present day

Nationalisation was enacted in 1972 when "a land reform programme was introduced based on the objectives of maximising agricultural production and employment and reducing inequalities in
wealth and income".[81] Under the Land Reform Law, No. 1 of 1972,
a ceiling was placed on the private (non-corporate) ownership of
25 acres for paddy and 50 acres for other categories of land.[82]
In 1975 the scope of the reform was extended under the Land Reform
(Amendment) Law, No. 39 of 1975. It was under this that plantations owned by local and foreign public companies were brought under
state control.[83] In all, these acquisitions comprised 63 per cent
of tea lands, 30 per cent of rubber and 10 per cent of the total
coconut acreage of the country.[84]

Since nationalisation the organisation of the plantation sector
has again undergone changes. After the reforms the land acquired
was placed under one of three kinds of management. There were
the two State Corporations - the Sri Lanka State Plantations Corporation and the Janatha Estates Development Board (the latter
started in April 1976 after the second stage of the takeover) -
which followed the pattern established under companies and agency
houses. A small proportion of the land was given to individual
villagers, and the rest was placed under various types of co-
operative organisations (the up-country Co-operative Estates,
Usawasama, the Land Reform Co-operatives, Janawasa, the Electoral
Co-operatives, and a number of other co-operative farms). The
Usawasama were established with the aim of developing co-operative
management. The Electoral Co-operatives and the Janawasa were
also attempts to introduce a new form of management, the former
being placed under the control of local politicians and the latter
based on collective responsibility. The Usawasama failed, and
the Electoral Co-operatives became little more than an avenue for
personal gain. The workers gained nothing in the process, and in
the majority of cases they had to forgo wages and other benefits
on the grounds that the estates were said to have been run at a loss.
The Janawasa emphasised the principle of collective ownership, and
in a few cases they were more successful in improving the conditions
of the labour force.[85]

The area under these various bodies changed over the years as
several reorganisations were attempted. By 1976, the two main
State Corporations controlled some 47 per cent of the alienated land.

With the change of Government in 1977 the Electoral Co-operatives
and the Usawasama were removed, and the large estates under the
Janawasama Commission were handed over to the Sri Lanka State Plantation Corporation and the Janatha Estates Development Board. Further reorganisation was later considered to be necessary,[86] and
the two boards were recently made into separate ministries and
placed under the direct control of the President of the country.
Decentralisation was also attempted in 1980 with the reorganisation
of both bodies on a regional basis. Both were divided into four
regional boards which were then granted a certain autonomy on the
grounds that "250,000 acres each are far too unwieldy for efficient
management".[87] How far all these changes have led to a restructuring
of estate management and to changes in management practices from
the pre-reform days is difficult to assess, but the evidence would
seem to suggest that they have changed very little. The use of
hierarchical and authoritarian structures is often said to be the
only way that the estate sector can drag itself out of its relative
stagnation, and strict discipline and careful supervision tend to
be given greater priority than negotiation. Given the increased
strength of the trade union movement, these practices cannot be
so rigidly adhered to as in the past; however, in the absence
of an alternative model the management still tends to retain and
to maintain the old standards, old attitudes and old values as to
what is "good" and what is "bad".[88]

Since nationalisation there has been stagnation or decline in
the production of the three main estate crops. This has been
quite pronounced in the case of tea; rubber output has been lower
than expected;[89] and there has been a sharp decline in coconut
production. The poor performance of the tea industry has been
attributed to "adverse weather conditions, continuing management
problems in the plantation sector, and the diversion to other crops
of some of the tea lands vested in the National Agricultural Diversi-
fication and Settlement Authority".[90] The most stagnant production
in the rubber industry is in turn attributed to "grossly inadequate
replanting in the past".[91] Coconut production was affected by
drought conditions and the cyclone in 1978. Be this as it may,
these factors do not explain the fact that output has failed even
to reach 1972 levels.

The period from 1972 to 1977 was also one of serious difficulties for estate labour. The repatriation process (reviewed in
1973) speeded up and in practice this often placed individual workers

in a far worse situation than that which they had faced while on the estate.[92]   Secondly, the estates themselves faced a shortage of food between 1972 and 1975, even though the trade unions were actively protesting this situation.[93]   As a consequence of this (and of the more general economic decline of the estate sector) total employment fell, although by far the greater part of the reduction was amongst the Tamils, many of whom were in fact repatriated.[94]

After 1977, when the UNP Government came into power, they embarked on an active policy designed to increase employment on the estates as a means of tackling the unemployment problem in the surrounding areas.   This policy, although it has been operating only for a short time, has had the effect of creating an excess labour situation on most coconut and rubber estates in the low- and mid-country.   The former have attempted to diversify in an effort to provide more work for the additional labour that has been imposed on them, and the rubber estates have often been confronted with little choice but to suffer a drop in profitability.   In contrast, tea estates located in the up-country areas were unable to find sufficient labour to replace the Indians who were steadily repatriated.   Almost the entire increase in Sinhalese labour on tea estates was comprised of females from neighbouring villages.   In 1977 the female workers on tea, rubber and coconut plantations constituted 51.1 per cent of the total labour force.[95]

The plantation worker has been given a certain degree of recognition by the fact that the President of the Ceylon Workers' Congress (the name adopted by the Ceylon Indian Congress in 1950 and which still is the largest union on the estates) became a Cabinet Minister in 1977 (Mr. Thondaman).   Other trade unions have been gaining support,[96] and the UNP trade union (the Lanka Jathika Estate Workers Union) has been slowly coming to prominence in recent years.   There have been some attempts to organise workers on coconut estates, but so far nothing significant has emerged.   The importance of casual labour has made it more difficult to organise these people, and has proved a serious obstacle to the trade union movement.

Conclusions

To summarise, historical analysis of the emerging plantation economy reflects both continuity and change. The basic form of the plantation as a unit of production had its antecedents in the experience in other areas, while the more detailed characterisation of the Sri Lankan case was heavily influenced by the specificities and peculiarities of that situation. In that respect there are five main points that can be raised by way of conclusion:

1. The basic organisational form and the division of labour on Sri Lankan plantations reflected a considerable degree of continuity with earlier British experience in the Caribbean. These characteristics were carried over to Sri Lanka for several reasons. They came under the same colonial power, eager to encourage investment along plantation lines wherever this seemed the most lucrative form of production. Following the abolition of slavery, indentured labour was introduced both in the Caribbean and in other areas, and it was a solution to the recurrent and perennial problem of labour supply which British investors and colonial governments knew and with which they were familiar. Traditional patriarchal and hierarchical forms of labour organisation were carried on into this later variation. It was found quite efficient to retain "non-capitalist" forms of labour control and to use them within the context of a capitalist structure. Racist and sexist ideologies found expression in this "new form of slavery" in the use of caste and in the reinforcement of traditional views which emphasised the inferiority of women.

2. Having emphasised this continuity, however, the point must also be made that there were several reasons why "adjustments" occurred in the transplantation of this model to the Sri Lankan setting. One of the simplest, but in many ways one of the most profound reasons, lay in the fact that very different crops were involved. Different crops meant different labour requirements, as a result of which the "rational" use of labour came to imply different patterns of labour migration and labour contracting and different ideas about how to minimise labour costs. This is reflected in the shift from seasonal to permanent labour, a shift to longer-term contracts, and to the use of female labour as cheap labour in time-consuming and

labour-intensive tasks. These shifts were a response to the changing labour needs of a series of crops, resulting in a bit by bit modification of labour management techniques within an established "Sri Lankan pattern of recruitment".

3. Again, once the Sri Lankan plantations had been founded, they became dependent upon the vagaries of the international market, and the management's response to changing economic conditions had implications in terms of its dealings with workers. At least until independence, the plantation sector dominated and guided the growth of the Sri Lankan economy, but increasingly it was controlled by corporate interests outside the country whose main concern was with profitability and not with the labour. In times of difficulty it was often the workers who had to suffer for this. During the depression, in the period between independence and nationalisation and even in the post-nationalisation period, external constraints imposed a series of limitations upon the industry and this resulted in unemployment, falling or stagnant wages.

4. Fourthly, the plantations were part and parcel of the rest of the economy. As was the case elsewhere in earlier periods Sri Lankan plantations were by no means enclaves unrelated to the rest of colonial society. On the contrary, they were in practice a very real part of it, exerting an influence and yet at the same time being influenced by it. Historically, they have encroached on peasant holdings creating at times landlessness and poverty. At the same time the priority they received under the colonial government had often a detrimental effect on the other sectors of the economy. They also were a symbol of the colonial power and have faced the aggression from the Sri Lankans both historically and in the post-independence period. As such, the development of the estate sector closely affected the rest of the economy.

5. However, for all of this there is no doubt one of the most important factors that shaped patterns of labour control on Sri Lankan plantations was the social background and social situation of the workers involved. The pattern of recruitment, caste differences amongst Tamils and the existing ideology within these communities concerning women were used historically to "good" effect by plantation management. Whether

consciously as in the case of the earlier planters, or as a
matter carrying on proven and accepted patterns of life and
work, this dimension had a strong influence on the concrete
form that Sri Lankan plantation took.   The social background
of these workers has been and still is of considerable importance for an understanding of the position of Sri Lankan plantation workers and particularly of women workers, and it is
to this that attention will now be turned.

Notes

[1] References can be found to earlier plantations in Sri Lanka:
the Dutch introduced State sponsored plantations in the second half
of the eighteenth century (D.M. Forrest: A Hundred years of Ceylon
tea (London, Chatto and Windus, 1967), p. 27) and coconut plantations
appear to date even further back to A.D. 589 (Report of the Coconut
Commission (Colombo, 1949), Sessional Paper No. XII of 1949, pp. 6-9).
However, such enterprises had little or no impact on the structure
of the rest of the economy.

[2] A.C.L. Ameer Ali: Peasant agriculture in Ceylon 1833-1893
(M. Phil. Thesis, London School of Economics, May 1970), p. 67;
and I.H. van den Driesen, "Plantation agriculture and land sales
policy in Ceylon, the first phase 1836-1886" (Part I), in University
of Ceylon Review (Colombo), Jan. 1956, Vol. XIV, No. 1.

[3] This resulted in the spread of plantation production of coffee
during this period, for example to Brazil, W. Dean: Rio Claro: a
Brazilian plantation system 1820-1920 (Stanford, Stanford University
Press, 1976).

[4] I.H. van den Driesen: "Coffee cultivation in Ceylon" (in
two parts), in Ceylon Historical Journal, 1954, p. 42f and p. 152f.

[5] D.R. Snodgrass: Ceylon: an export economy in transition
(Homewood (Illinois), Richard D. Irwin Inc. for the Economic Growth
Centre, Yale University, 1966), p. 19; M. Roberts and L.A. Wickre-
meratne: "Export agriculture in the nineteenth century" in K.M. de
Silva (eds.): University of Ceylon History of Ceylon (Colombo,
University of Ceylon Press Board, 1973), Vol. III, pp. 94-97.

[6] Van den Driesen op.cit. 1956, p. 8.

[7] ibid.

[8] Sir Edward Jackson: Report of a commission on immigration
into Ceylon (Colombo, 1938), Sessional Paper No. 3, p. 24.

[9] Roberts and Wickremeratne, op. cit., p. 99.

[10] Monetarisation in practice made inroads into this.

[11] Dates given for this initial recruitment are contradictory.
Lakshman de Mel and D.M. Forrest note that the first planter to
recruit this sort of labour was Bird in 1844 (L. de Mel: The evolution of industrial relations in Ceylon with special reference to

the plantations (Geneva, Institute for Labour Studies, 1972), p. 1;
and Forrest, op. cit., p. 41). Jayawardena dates this recruitment
from 1825 onwards (K. Jayawardena: The rise of the labour movement
in Ceylon (Durham (North Carolina), Duke University Press, 1972),
p. 16), while Snodgrass, based on Ferguson and others suggests that
large-scale migration had already begun by 1839 (Snodgrass, op. cit.,
1966, p. 24, and J. Ferguson: The Ceylon Directory for 1874 (Colombo,
1874), p. 244). Since coffee plantations were of no real significance before the late 1830s or early 1840s (Ameer Ali, op. cit.,
p. 67f), 1839 stands out as the most reasonable date at which to
begin an analysis of estate labour.

[12] See Report and proceedings of the Labour Commission (headed
by Sir Hugh Clifford), (Colombo, 1908), pp. vii-viii.

[13] For details of the medical examination and the registration
see S.E.N. Nicholas: Estate labour and legal guide (Colombo,
C.A.P. Press, 1927), p. 14f. On the hardships of the journey see
Administration reports for 1899, Report of the Medical Officer,
p. A2 and pp. 12-18; The Times of Ceylon supplement to mark the
Ceylon Tea Century, 1967, p. 66; and Jayawardena, op. cit., p. 17.

[14] Using data on land sales for this period given by van den
Driesen, where he says that the average sale to a European between
1833 and 1860 was 97 acres (I.H. van den Driesen: The economic
history of Ceylon in the nineteenth century, Vol. I, Plantations,
land and capital (unpublished English manuscript of a Sinhalese
book, 1961), p. 125), Snodgrass suggests that this be taken as
"a first approximation of the size of the average coffee plantation"
(Snodgrass, op. cit., 1966, p. 23).

[15] Roberts and Wickremeratne, op. cit., p. 96.

[16] This description of the "Kangany system" and the general
structure of labour relies heavily on the Report and proceedings
of the Labour Commission, op. cit.

[17] Report and proceedings of the Labour Commission, op. cit.
p. vii, para. 6.

[18] ibid., p. ix.

[19] This method of shifting labour from estate to estate had come
under criticism from the earliest days. It was seen as "the evil
that lies at the root of most of the labour troubles" (ibid.,
para. 30). The way that the kanganies bettered their economic
position was by threatening to remove gangs of coolies to another
estate unless further cash advances were immediately paid. The
superintendent then had to decide if he would pay or suffer the
loss of labour. In the latter case, the kangany would approach
the superintendent of another estate which was known to have a labour
shortage and to offer his gangs on payment of their outstanding
liabilities as laid out in the tundu plus in addition some other
advance. (ibid.)

[20] Report and proceedings of the Labour Commission, op. cit.

[21] Jayawardena, op. cit., p. 17.

[22] ibid.

[23] Jayaraman observed that the basis of these subkangany groups was homogeneity in terms of caste and kinship. Such 'gangs' tended to preserve traditional norms and customs, reinforcing at the same time value and respect for the authority of those who were on a higher level of the existing hierarchy (Jayaraman op. cit. 1975, pp. 57-64).

[24] Jayawardena op. cit. 1972, p. 20.

[25] M. Roberts: "The master-servant laws of 1841 and the 1960s and immigrant labour in Ceylon", in The Ceylon Journal of Historical and Social Studies (Peradeniya), 1965, Vol. 8.

[26] Sir James Emerson Tennent to Earl Grey, Co. 54/235, No. 6 21 Apr. 1848.

[27] Report on the working of the Indian Emigration Act, 1932, p. 18.

[28] The various "acceptable" ways of constructing line rooms so as not to offend the traditional prejudices of the workers are detailed in L. Green: The planter's book of caste and custom (Colombo, The Times of Ceylon Company Ltd. and London, Blackfriars House, 1925), see chapter on housing. Interviews with the superintendents confirmed this picture, though they attributed it to the fact that the kangany's advice was generally accepted, and not to any conscious attempt on the part of management to maintain these features.

[29] See van den Driesen, op. cit.

[30] Ameer Ali, op. cit.

[31] See L.A. Wickremeratne: "The development of transportation in Ceylon 1800-1947", in de Silva, op. cit., pp. 303-316.

[32] Report of the Kandyan Peasantry Commission, Sessional Paper XVIII of 1951, p. 70, para. 219. In 1861 the Government took steps to provide four vessels for the transport of Indian labour from Rameswarem to Mannar; in 1866 an annual subsidy was granted for 3 years to a company in Bombay for regularly transporting workers from South Indian ports to Colombo.

[33] See A.C.M. Ameer Ali: "Rice and irrigation in nineteenth century Sri Lanka", in The Ceylon Historical Journal (Dahiwala), Oct. 1978, Vol. XXV, Nos. 1-4.

[34] D. Dunham: Land, plantations and peasants in Sri Lankan development: the period prior to 1900 (The Hague, Institute of Social Studies, 1980).

[35] Snodgrass, op. cit. 1966, p. 19.

[36] This can be observed from the following table:

Year	Area (000/acres)	Exports (000/cwt)	Prices (sh/cwt)
1845-49	51	260	39.8
1850-54	59	344	42.5
1855-59	138	537	49.6
1860-64	199	615	52.2
1865-69	243	939	54.0

Source: Snodgrass: op. cit. table 2-1; and van den Driesen, op. cit.

[37] In the 1870s, over two-thirds of the estates in operation were owned by individuals while the rest were under corporate ownership. In addition, several individual owners left the management of their estates to agency houses. See Snodgrass, op. cit., p. 27, and Roberts and Wickremeratne, op. cit. pp. 96-97.

[38] Snodgrass, op. cit., p. 21. For details of trends in the 1870s see G. Corea: The instability of an export economy (Colombo, Marga Institute, 1975), and Roberts and Wickremeratne, op, cit., p. 102.

[39] "The cultivation of tea was taken up by those coffee planters who were able to outlast the coffee disaster", comment by Kotawala, Legislative Council Debates, 20 Apr. 1933, p. 693. "Many of the plantations were deserted, the capitalists took fright, superintendents were thrown out of employment and set off to other countries. There was a regular migration to Northern Australia, Fiji, Borneo, the Straits, California, Florida, Burma and elsewhere. I should say that out of 1,700 planters we lost at least 400 in this way". J. Ferguson: Ceylon in the Jubilee Year (London 1887), p. 330.

[40] A significant upswing in prices occurred in the period 1900-1912 when supply fell far short of the demand of rubber. See Wickremeratne op. cit. 1973, pp. 433-434.

[41] Snodgrass, op. cit., p. 38, and Wickremeratne, op. cit., p. 430f.

[42] Snodgrass, op. cit., Statistical Appendix, Table A-37.

[43] By 1910 rubber had already replaced coconut products as the largest export item after tea (Wickremeratne, op. cit., p. 428). For the importance of rubber vis-à-vis tea and coconuts see Snodgrass, op. cit., Statistical Appendix, Table A52. In 1913 the value of tea exports was Rs. 87.8 million that of rubber Rs. 61.2 million and that of coconut oil, copra and dessicated coconut Rs. 45.6 million. Rubber became the largest source of foreign exchange in 1917, when the value of its exports exceeded even that of tea. In 1919 and 1920 there was a similar situation, but after that it took a second place to tea.

[44] Snodgrass, op. cit., p. 42. The proportion was roughly 40 per cent in the 1930s.

[45] Ordinance no. 14 of 1854 allowed planters to enter into written contracts for up to a year. It was only under Ordinance No. 20 of 1865 that contracts entered in India for a maximum period of 3 years were made legally binding in Sri Lanka, a feature that had been specifically refused earlier. See Roberts op. cit. 1965, p. 32. For the political debate surrounding policies of the British Crown to the use of "indentured labour" in British Colonies see A. H. Adamson: Sugar without slaves: the political economy of British Guiana, 1838-1904 (Yale University Press, New Haven and London, 1972), pp. 41-54.

[46] The proportion of females to males increased substantially from the 1860s. See Jayaraman op. cit., 1975, p. 28f. Governor's Despatch Mis, No. 6 of 21 Apr. 1847 op. cit., p. 207.

47 During the years from 1843 to 1880 a total of 275,418 Indian
workers came into the country and 187,062 returned home, leaving
a residual population of 88,356.   Between 1891 and 1930 a total
of 468,132 came and 320,744 left, leaving a residual population of
147,388.   (Panditaratne and Selvanayagam, op. cit., pp. 289-290.)

48 Ferguson's Ceylon Directory for 1866-68 has noted the fact
that while female labour (excluding child labour) constituted only
2.6 per cent of the total labour force in 1843, this had increased
to 26.87 per cent in 1866.   (Ferguson's Ceylon Directory, 1866-1868,
p. 183 and Appendix 2.)   From then on the proportion of female
labour substantially increased to exceed the number of males working
in this sector (Employment Survey, Department of Labour, 1977, p. 12).

49 There are references (as mentioned earlier) to coconut plantations existing as early as A.D. 589 and several others indicating
the long history of this crop in Sri Lanka.   See Report of the
Coconut Commission, op. cit., pp. 6-9.

50 It is estimated that one man is necessary for 8-10 acres on
the coconut plantation.   (See Land reform and the development of
coconut lands (Agrarian Research and Training Institute, Colombo,
1977), p. 1).   The tea labour requirement is about 1.25 men per
acre and rubber 0.7 men per acre.

51 Roberts and Wickremeratne, op. cit., p. 103.

52 Roberts and Wickremeratne, op. cit.   The Ceylon Directories
of 1871-72 and 1880-81 suggest that 66-71 per cent of the coconut
plantations in non-European hands were owned by low country Sinhalese
and 13-28 per cent by Ceylon Tamils.

53 At the height of the war 90 per cent of Sri Lanka's output
was sold at frozen prices (Snodgrass op. cit. 1966, p. 34).   As
a result, most tea estates were operating at a loss, given the
increasing costs of production and excise duty.   Some estates were
losing as much as ten cents a pound, and in many parts of the island
as many as half of the estates were said to have been abandoned.
See Legislative Council Debates, 1920-21, pp. 249-51 (Debate on the
export on tea).

54 Coconut oil which had hitherto accounted for the major part
of coconut exports by value declined in importance.

55 Output restriction schemes were affected in the tea and
rubber industries and these helped to push prices up initially.

56 See the proposals for the restriction of rubber, Legislative
Council Debates, 15 Feb. 1933, pp. 257-259 and 28 Mar. pp. 608-610.
According to the Director of Agriculture some 40 per cent of the
tappable area was left untapped in 1932 and about half of the Indian
workers who had been employed in 1931 had by then been laid off
(P.T. Bauer: The rubber industry (Cambridge, Mass. 1948), p. 54)
as prices "fell toward the vanishing point" (Snodgrass op. cit.
1966, p. 40).

57 The price was often restored to pre-depression levels by the
International Tea Regulation Scheme, under which the major tea pro-
ducing countries (India, Sri Lanka and the Netherlands East Indies)
agreed among themselves appropriate levels of production in order
to maintain a favourable price in the international market.   This
scheme was successively executed until the beginning of the 1939-45
war.

[58] The reductions occurred in May 1931, December 1931 and May 1933. They implied a money wage reduction of some 24 per cent in the up-country estates, 28 per cent in the mid-country estates and 30 per cent in the low-country estates in the course of this period. See Corea, op. cit., p. 90.

[59] The Indian workforce declined from 563,000 to 434,000 and the non-Indian from 57,000 to 47,000.

[60] From 100,000 to 50,000.

[61] Corea, op. cit., p. 91. Among the staff that were unemployed were 434 superintendents and assistant superintendents, 550 conductors, 334 clerks and 159 dispensers. Quoted in Corea, op. cit., from Report on unemployment in Ceylon (Colombo, 1937), Sessional Papers No. VII, Chapter I, p. 5.

[62] Contracts were to be entered into for the purchase of Sri Lanka's exports at "fair" prices for bulk delivery to the United Kingdom. Prices were initially set at pre-war levels but were later adjusted to compensate the producers (to some extent) for the rise in the cost of production.

[63] See Corea, op. cit., p. 171, and Snodgrass, op. cit., p. 75.

[64] The export price index moved from 100 to 179 between 1939 and 1945, while the import price index moved from 100 to 323 in the same period.

[65] The Rubber Commissioner who was both an agent of the British Ministry and an official of the colonial Government fixed a price that was likely to secure as large an output as possible. Since the gestation period for rubber was at least five to seven years, "slaughter tapping" (i.e. tapping the tree too often and too deep to increase its yield) was resorted to in order to obtain short term results. In the long run, this killed the tree.

[66] Ordinance No. 17 of 1880 (commonly known as the Medical Aid Ordinance) made provisions for minimal medical assistance to be provided for estate workers. This was totally inadequate and the death rate was so high that a Mortality Commission was appointed in 1893 to look into the matter. The latter was very critical of the medical facilities available on the estates. (See District Hospital Mortality Commission Report (Sessional Paper No. II, Colombo 1893). Although some improvement was attempted, it was still very inadequate.

[67] It was because of this that the Medical Wants Ordinance and the Diseases Ordinance of 1912 were passed. Maternity benefits of 75 cents per week and two measures of rice for four weeks were laid down under the former Ordinance. See 25 years of labour progress in Ceylon (Department of Labour, Colombo 1948), p. 72. One of the first Ceylonese nationalists who expressed concern openly was Ponnambatam Asurachalam, who between 1913 and 1922 led a campaign against the wages and conditions on plantations (Jayawardena op. cit. 1972, p. 337).

[68] In 1909 the worker was made immune from arrest in civil cases while Ordinance No. 43 of 1921 did away with penal clauses and the "tundu" system. See "The law relating to Indian Labourers", in Hansard 1926, Vol. III, pp. 1448-1498.

[69] Natesa Aiyar wrote Planter Raj which was considered "an inflammatory pamphlet attacking the planters. It gave a grim description of working conditions on plantations" (Jayawardena, op. cit., p. 341).

[70] See "The Law relating to Indian Labourers" op. cit., passim, and "Cooly Lines on Ceylon Estates", in Legislative council debates (Colombo, Sri Lanka National Archives, 24 Feb. 1927), p. 357f.

[71] See Jayawardena, op. cit., pp. 347-354. This ordinance "provided for the setting up of plantation wages boards in revenue districts composed of a chairman, a public officer, two members representing the employers, and two representing the workers. The members were to hold office for three years and were to fix minimum rates of wages of plantations within the jurisdiction of the board. The Ordinance also made provision for the payment of monthly wages before the tenth day of the following month. The whole amount of wages (apart from legal deductions for rice, etc.) had to be paid directly to the worker himself. The employer also had to comply with regulations regarding discharges and immigration certificates of workers. It was further stipulated that no child under the age of ten should be allowed to work on plantations" (ibid., p. 349).

[72] See earlier discussion.

[73] Between 1926 and 1928 Natesa Aiyar and A.E. Goonesinha had worked together. They had jointly edited the radical paper Forward which highlighted the contradictions that existed at national and international level. Aiyar was involved with trade union activity of the Ceylon Labour Union becoming its vice-president for a short period. Goonesinha, however, did not extend his trade union activities to the plantation sector. It was mainly on this issue that the rift emerged between them and it was to be maintained throughout the depression period.

[74] Gandhi visited the island in 1927 and Nehru came in 1931. Nehru was vocal in the protest against the reduction of the minimum wage for the plantation workers.

[75] The membership of the Ceylon Indian Congress during this period rose as follows:

Year	Membership
1940-41	96,000
1945-46	108,000
1946-47	117,000

Source: "Estate labour", Economic review, People's Bank Publication, Colombo, March 1980, p. 11.

[76] ibid.

[77] In the years from 1946-1950 the average number of strikes annually was 64, the average number of workers involved annually was 110,085 and the average number of man-days lost was 209,720. The corresponding figures for the rest of the island were 39; 18,426; and 166,946 respectively. (R. Kearney: Trade unions and politics in Ceylon (New Delhi, Thomson Press, (India) Ltd.), and Berkeley, University of California Press, 1971), Table 5.

[78] Kearney observes that "estate strikes in this period frequently were brief, often abrupt, eruptions which represented demon-
strations of protest and discontent, but because of the lack of
bargaining strength and the relatively weak organisation of estate
labour they generally were not a serious contest of strength with
employers intended to win specific demands". (Kearney, op. cit.,
p. 35). On the other hand the protests against disenfranchisement
in 1948-49 were long and often protracted. See Economic Review,
op. cit., Mar. 1980, p. 5; and Ceylon Administrative Reports for
1949, Section (c) F 11 and F 12, where there are two cases of pro-
longed strikes on account of the estate management refusing to
confer with the unions (strikes on the Roeberry Group estate, Madul-
sima, and on Agrakande estate, Lindula). The workers realised
the power of their bargaining position and if the demands were a
little less radical they still had the potential of drawing attention
to the difficulties on their situation.

[79] Economic Review, op. cit., Mar. 1980, pp. 5-6.

[80] See Economic and social development of Ceylon: a survey,
presented to Parliament by Hon. M.D. Jayawardena, Minister of
Finance, 1955, p. 30.

[81] G.H. Peiris: "Land reform and agrarian change in Sri Lanka",
in Modern Asian Studies (Cambridge and New York, 1978), Vol. 12,
No. 4.

[82] This also provided for the establishment of a land reform
commission to implement the reform. Other legislation relating
to this land reform includes the Estates (Control and Transfer)
Act No. 2 of 1972, The State Agricultural Corporation Act No. 11
of 1972, The Agricultural Productivity Law No. 2 of 1972 and the
Agricultural Lands Law No. 42 of 1973.

[83] Under the former the Government acquired 563,422 acres of
which tea, rubber and coconut constituted nearly 60 per cent (tea
139,354 acres, rubber 82,563 acres, and coconut 112,523 acres).
In the second phase in 1975 a further 417,975 acres were acquired,
of which tea, rubber and coconut accounted for 81 per cent (tea
237,592 acres, rubber 94,853 acres and coconut 6,406 acres). Source:
Land Reform Commission.

[84] The area retained was often above the legal maximum. Richards
for example has calculated that "the average over 50 acre holding
remained between 70 and 80 acres after the land reform". P. Richards:
"Comment on Isenman, 'Basic Needs: the case of Sri Lanka'", in
World Development (Oxford, 1981) Vol. 9, No. 2.

[85] A janawasa was defined as a "settlement established on the
principles of collective ownership and self-management". The socio-
economic aspects of this form of management has been examined in
a study of Joint farming systems in Sri Lanka by N. Shanmugaratnam
(unpublished thesis, University of Colombo, 1979).

[86] This was done "with a view to provide better management
and a more balanced mix of lands under each of them". Ronnie de
Mel, Minister of Finance, "History of Finance", in Budget Speech
for 1980, National State Assembly Debates, 14 Nov. 1979.

[87] ibid.

[88] Unlike "the good old days", as the pre-reform period is often termed, the management is no longer compensated according to performance. The superintendent who makes a profit is no better paid than the one working on an estate that is making a loss. This has caused serious problems of disincentives in the plantation industry and the departure of management personnel to more rewarding concerns.

[89] Under the Rubber Replanting Subsidy Scheme an annual rate of replanting of 3 per cent to 4 per cent of the total rubber acreage was maintained in the 1960s, but the increased output expected from this in the 1970s was not to materialise.

[90] Budget Speech for 1980, op. cit. 1979.

[91] ibid.

[92] See "Immigrants in their Homeland", in Economic and Political Weekly, 22 Feb. 1975, pp. 353-356, and A report on the survey of repatriates from Sri Lanka 1980 (Centre for Research on New International Economic order, Madras, 1980).

[93] The Ceylon Workers Congress participated in 297 strikes in this period out of which 119 were related to food shortages.

[94] See Statistical Abstracts 1977, Table 53, p. 120. The number of Indian and Sinhalese workers in 1972 were 364,841 and 123,497 respectively. The corresponding figures for 1976 are 252,246 and 111,106.

[95] Employment Survey (Department of Labour), 1977, p. 12.

[96] The other main trade unions are the Democratic Workers' Congress, the Ceylon Planters' Workers Union, the Lanka Jathika Estate Workers' Union.

Chapter 3

THE SOCIAL BACKGROUND OF PLANTATION LABOUR AND
AND ITS IMPLICATIONS FOR WOMEN

Workers on the Sri Lankan estates generally belong to one of
two distinct communities. They are either Tamil, originating from
Tamil-Nadu in India (the vast majority) or they are from the
Sinhalese villages located along the outskirts of the estates.
The norms and accepted behaviour patterns in these two communities
influence the attitudes of the estate labour force to particular
forms of labour organisation and labour control and as such they are
important for an understanding of the prevailing situation and of
the way in which it has emerged.

The social background of these workers is also relevant for
an understanding of the particular roles and status which women
assume and of why they are inclined to (or forced to) accept their
lot. The respective backgrounds of these two communities has been
such that they have ascribed particular roles to women; they
reflected attitudes which were most clearly expressed in traditional
rules governing the inheritance of property and relations to kin,
and designed to perpetuate existing patterns of property and power.
These were in turn sustained by an ideology in which men were
superior and which was both strong and influential in daily life.

Regardless of their community, estate workers were very aware
of traditional norms, practices and expectations and even if they
themselves had little wealth they lived in a community in which some
had more and used "tradition" in order to maintain the distinctions
that did occur. They could not therefore immediately do away with
rights and duties that were part and parcel of "traditions", power
structures and ways of life. And yet the way in which these
practices were observed varied according to the social and economic
status of particular groups within their community, to change
influencing their community as a whole, and to the nature of their
integration into the estate workforce. The estate, as we have
seen, reinforced traditional features (such as differences in
caste) in as far as they furthered its interests in labour control.
But in time changes also occurred in the work situation (such as
trade unionisation) which began to have an impact on traditional
structures.

This chapter is concerned with the analysis of these structures: it will examine the various social forces that have played an important role in shaping the situation of both Tamil and Sinhalese workers on Sri Lankan estates, paying attention to their implications for women. More specifically, it will concentrate on four main themes reflecting key areas for an understanding of the position of female labour:

(1) the integration of the Tamil labour force into the estates and the resulting sanskritisation and subsequent loss of freedom for women;

(2) the integration of Sinhalese workers and the social and economic independence of these women;

(3) the similarity between Tamil and Sinhalese kinship structures and mechanisms of social control with regard to the production and reproduction activities of women; and

(4) inroads made into traditional social structure as a result of changes taking place outside.

The integration of Tamil workers into the estates

Most of the Indian population came (as we have noted) from the districts of Trichinopoly, Salem and Tanjore (over 60 per cent).[1] However, there were also sizeable contributions from Madura, Ramnad, Pudakottai, North and South Arcot, Chingleput, Tinnevelly and Coimbatore. These were areas characterised by a strong caste-oriented society where the institution of caste or jati determined prevailing norms and behaviour patterns as reflected in their day-to-day customs and essential ceremonies.

The caste system in India has long been described by many authorities.[2] Indian social life was and still is largely articulated through the caste system, and most social organisations related to economic, political or educational affairs tend to be affected by caste considerations. In general we can say that the caste was an endogamous group, originally implying an ascribed occupation,[3] and ranked in a hierarchical order. Within the Indian context there are four main divisions of caste:

(1) the Brahmins - the priests;

(2) the Kshatriyas - the warriors and the military;

(3) the Vaishyas or Bannians - the traders; and

(4) the Sudras - the cultivators.

Below them come the so-called "outcastes" or Adi-Dravidas.[4]

Each of these groups has several subdivisions; each subdivi-
sion is in turn an endogamous group and a person acquires membership
of a caste group solely by birth.   The hierarchical order to these
castes follows the pattern that is given above.

The two main divisions that are to be found on the Sri Lankan
estates are the Sudras and the Adi-Dravidas.   The former include
the Vellelans, Kallans, Ahambadiyans, Ambalakaran and the Maravans.
The Adi-Dravida groups included the Pallans, Parayans, the Valluvans
and the Chakkiliyans.   Far more divisions (or subdivisions) have
been noted and their characteristics recorded,[5] but for our study
it is sufficient to note that these people came from relatively low
castes within the Indian caste system and that these were the main
socio-cultural groups.

There are several studies to show that the notions of "pollution"
and "purity", so intrinsic to Indian caste ideology, were far less
rigidly observed amongst the lower castes in India.[6]   The Sudras
and Adi-Dravidas were less concerned with religious rituals and
ceremonies.   As far as women from these groups were concerned, their
"traditional" professions as cultivators or scavengers created for
them a more independent situation and a more equal position vis-à-vis
men of the same subcaste.   There was little male domination in this
situation.   Inter-caste marriages were more widely accepted, extramarital sexual relationships were common and in the case of the
Adi-Dravidas this trend was even more pronounced than amongst the
Sudra people.

On the other hand, as plantation workers, the Sudra subcastes
made a very conscious attempt to preserve the conservative caste
system, to reintroduce and to reconstruct a pyramid of caste power
with themselves at the top (as the people who in the Sri Lankan
context had the highest caste).   Castes and subcastes in this
truncated structure experienced in effect an upward mobility -
generally known as a process of Sanskritisation.   This situation
resulted from and was stimulated by the plantation system and by
the way in which it recruited and organised its labour force.
Firstly, the pattern of migration under the supervision of a
kangany, the tendency for migration to take place in families or

with relatives, and the eventual normalisation of the sex composition of the immigrant labour (as described in Chapter 2), served to
make the preservation of caste identity that much easier.   Secondly,
when they arrived on the estate, their location was such that they
were isolated from the rest of Sri Lankan society.   Even when they
touched, Sri Lanka had a social system which was "quasi-feudal" in
nature and by no means inimical to that of the Indians.[7]   Thirdly,
the formation of labour gangs under kanganies and subkanganies
tended to strengthen caste and kinship ties.[8]   Fourthly, the
estate owners had an interest in preserving caste and using the
ideology that lay behind it to control the worker and to maintain
a peaceful and stable labour force.   Caste differences were consciously exploited to create suspicion in the labour force, thereby
preventing effective labour organisation and they were also used as
a mechanism of labour control.   The kanganies used them in order
to maintain their own status and their own position.   Finally,
Tamil workers were not only geographically but also economically
and politically isolated.   They found themselves with little by way
of political representation and they were unable to find employment
outside the estates.   The result was that they were firmly confined
to their situation.

The caste differences between these workers were expressed
in a number of ways.   Living quarters, for example, were arranged
on the basis of caste.   Higher caste people disliked living in
the same lines as people of lower castes, or in some cases, even
to look upon them.[9]   The result was a concentration of a particular
caste or subcaste in one line or area and this kept awareness of
caste very much to the fore.   Religious ceremonies and festivals
were rigidly observed and these too had a very important caste
dimension.   If an Adi-Dravida cooked food at a festival, the
Sudras would simply refuse to eat it.   In the same way, hypergamous
marriages were strongly condemned and if the castes involved were
not structurally close, this could result in virtual ostracism for
the people concerned.   The notions of "pollution" and "purity"
assumed greater significance amongst Tamil community plantations
than they had held for these people when they were in India.

The social setting also had important consequences for the
position of women.   Inequality between men and women, which in an
"ideal" sense was an important feature of Hinduism, became even
more apparent in the lives of these people.   Their theological

beliefs had social and logical ramifications when it came to the activities and practices of the Hindus on these estates.[10] Festivals were in general important and even more so in the lives of the women because these were the only opportunities available to them for social contacts outside their plantation work. Religion became a more important part of their lives and the inequalities inherent in their religion became an even stronger means of control. Women could not set foot inside the temple's "sacred area" lest their action should pollute the gods. The important ceremonies that followed births were much more elaborate in the case of male than female children. A male child was always considered to be that much better. When girls reached puberty, this too was the subject of ceremony, but in the course of their first menstruation they were confined to a separate section of the house, lest they pollute the other family members.[11] The marriage ceremony emphasised the subservience of women,[12] and following a death,it was the men and not the women who accompanied the deceased to the graveyard.[13] All these points served to engrain a sense of woman's inferiority into the consciousness of the Tamil community. These rituals were rarely observed with such sex or caste segregation among the Sudras who lived in Tamil Nadu.

Secondly, the process of Sanskritisation had the effect of creating definite loss of freedom on the part of the woman.[14] As a Hindu family tried to emulate the ritual behaviour of higher castes, private ownership became increasingly relevant. The woman came more and more to be seen as the private property of her husband and subservient to him. The marriage became "sacred", and the woman had to observe a strict code of sexual behaviour. The process implied distinguishing one's self from other people, as a result of which the woman involved became more isolated and cut off from the rest of the community. By emphasising caste differences Sudra subcaste women began losing the freedom that they had earlier enjoyed not only in their daily social relations, but in their control of food, money and other resources.

Sudra women would be very particular to avoid alcohol and to participate in the various religious rituals. In contrast, women of lower castes often drank, their attitude in general was much more relaxed and they were less concerned with the need to follow very strict rituals. It is also interesting to note the attitude that they displayed to the men in their households. Though all

the women say that they hold their husbands in fear (bhayam),
there is a correlation between level in the caste hierarchy and the
degree of reticence that women display towards their men.   The
higher the caste the greater the reserve and respect they are
inclined to show.   Sudra women tend to be less free and more subservient to their husbands than women from the Pallans, Paraiyans
and the Chakkiliyans.   The latter tend to be much more open and
they often preferred to stand up and defend their own rights.   In
short, the process and nature and integration into the estate labour
force in kin groups and in subcaste groups led to a re-emergence
and reinforcement of caste ideology and caste power and to a loss
of freedom for women within their community.

The integration of Sinhalese labour into the estate

The other important section of the plantation labour force
has been the Sinhalese villagers who are now prominent on rubber
and coconut estates in the low-country areas.   Up-country, there
have always been far fewer Sinhalese working on the estates, and
it is only very recently (post 1977) that there has been any marked
increase in their numbers.

There are several important factors that have to be taken into
account with regard to the social background of these workers.
Firstly, they too were part of a caste system which predated
plantation agriculture and which also placed the woman in an
inferior position.   Secondly, while in the low-country areas
feudal caste relations were less pronounced, increasing commercialisation was creating a class of indigenous entrepreneurs who
had adopted notions of private property and these again stressed
very clearly the inferiority of women (discussed in Chapter 1).

Thirdly, the Sinhalese women who have more recently (since
1977) gained employment on the estates were from a stratum of village
society which was socially and economically marginalised.   Their
situation was such that their physical circumstances forced them
to survive independent of men and in their case their integration
into the estate labour force had the effect of giving them an
element of freedom from this society.   Each of these issues will
be examined in turn.

Since 1824, the year in which the first caste census was
taken, the Goyigama (the cultivator caste to which the highest
status is attached), has constituted more than 60 per cent of the
population.[15]   Though not strictly a part of the Buddhist religion
as it was in Hinduism, caste services had been demanded on a hierarchical basis, articulated around the interests of the higher
orders of the (landowning) Goyigama caste.   Single-caste villages
existed, particular services being performed when they were called
for by way of rent.   Caste ideology was therefore an important
feature in the lives of the Sinhalese in the village.

The implications of this for the position of women lay in the
fact that these caste values had an inherently patriarchal aspect
to them.   Women did not take part in administration; they depended
on their men for their contacts outside the family, and they were
given little place in the power structure of their own society.
They were considered a form of property or an appendage to the man
or to the caste in question.   Any behaviour on the part of the
woman which failed to meet the approval of the caste or of the man
in the household was strongly condemned as an indication of the
impurity she had imparted to the family name.   Instances have been
cited of cases where a high-caste woman ran away to live with a low-
caste man; the family reactions were such as to kill her believing
that by her death the stain on the family honour would be removed.[16]
Were a similar act committed by the man, then in all probability he
would at worst be ostracised by his family and by his own caste
group.   In neither case was such a liaison encouraged, but while
it was considered an act of individual rashness on the part of the
man (and wholeheartedly condemned), it became a matter of family
dishonour in the case of the woman, one that was in need of punishment
of the severest kind.[17]

In the case of the low-country areas, the rigidity of feudal
tenancy relations was moderated to a large extent by contact with
international trade and by a number of other external influences,[18]
and in many instances by the single caste village where there tended
to be less differentiation and power relations were formed on a
different basis.   In both these cases, that of foreign commercial
influence and that of the one-caste village, the net effect was to
ease the question of economic fortunes and political power from its
traditional caste basis with the emergence of new power "élites"
in the local society.[19]

Be as it may, these changes had little effect on the position
of women and certainly not on the division of labour within the
home or on attitudes towards them and towards men in their society.
The ideology of male superiority was not disturbed; it was simply
incorporated into the emerging system which saw the increasing
prevalence of the "nuclear" family as the unit of household production and reproduction.

Secondly, with the spread of commercialisation in the
twentieth century, there was increasing pauperisation as landlessness and unemployment became more widespread.   The extension of
plantations into mid- and low-country areas, population growth and
spread of monetarisation in the island all acted as important cata-
lysts in this, resulting in fragmentation, indebtedness and
disposession of land.[20]   A new landowning class began to emerge,
emphasising private property and identifying with Western thinking
and ideology.   As far as women were concerned this found expression
in the norms and structure of the "nuclear" family; female labour
was considered inferior, household activities were seen as "natural"
functions of women and this thinking dominated the power structure
and social controls at a village level.

Thirdly, with regard to the post-independence period (and
especially post-1977) the poorest sections of Sinhalese society
were confronted more and more with the need to find employment
and income.   If necessary, they were willing to move outside the
village and this gave rise to a situation where men - being mobile -
migrated to the cities or to other rural areas, leaving women behind
to look after their families with no support from their menfolk
whatsoever.   These constituted a large proportion of the Sinhalese
women who were found to be working on tea estates, despite the
difficulties involved and the taboos against it.   The social and
economic marginalisation of this class forced a break with the
traditional division of labour and customs (where the woman was
"protected").   Consequently, common-law marriages of a temporary
nature became common (the marriage laws preventing early marriages
encouraged this trend).

In short, the social background of the women in this sample
can be said to have had the following characteristics.   They were
almost invariably people from very poor backgrounds doing work to
which low status was generally attached.   Their family structure
preserved the normal distinctions in terms of the division of labour,

with the women primarily responsible for "household" tasks, which
included looking after the needs of the men and the children.
Socially, these people did not maintain a serious religious or
caste base influencing the way that they conducted their lives.
Marriages were founded more on individual choice than on arrangements made by the parents and the rigidity of the marriage was
itself not so strong. A number of marriages broke up or were
simply not formalised, the people involved preferring to live
together.

This was a pattern of life frowned upon by the rest of the
community. Society at large preserved traditional attitudes and
traditional customs that were inherently patriarchal, emphasising
male superiority. These people, because of their economic and
social marginality, rejected them, or at least were not so rigid,
because these norms had little to offer for them. The very fact
that they had to seek work outside the village forced on them a
certain break with traditional practices and with what had become
"the accepted" way of life. And as a result of this women in
particular were forced to become more independent vis-à-vis men of
their own caste.

The kinship relation of estate labour

The third theme mentioned at the outset of this chapter was
the similarity in the kinship relations of estate labour regardless
of the community from which they came and the idea that inherent
within them was a particular pattern of social control. A crucial
aspect of this as we shall see, is control of the production and
reproduction activities of women through the system of inheritance,
customs and ideology. Attention will now be turned to this
dimension.

Conventionally, estate Tamils have been considered as a
separate population with different values and customs from the
Sinhalese and they themselves would tend to say that they have no
connection with Sinhalese culture or traditions. And yet, a careful analysis of the kinship relations in their respective societies
reveals considerable affinity not only in terms of kinship structures,
descent, marriage, inheritance and other customs and institutions,
but even in as far as the actual terminology used.

In both cases, the basic unit of social organisation is the
nuclear family although bonds of kinship may also extend outside.
The latter comprise on a secondary level grandparents, brothers
and sisters of the parents and their children, on a tertiary level
other relatives (particularly on the male side), and on a quarter-
nary level other members of their caste or subcaste as the case may
be.[21]   Secondly, sets of relationships (mother's brother, father-
in-law and father's sister's husband or younger brothers and younger
male parallel cousins) are grouped together and referred to by the
same term implying the same duties and obligations.[22]

In both cases, descent is traced from father to son.[23]
Marriages are predominantly virilocal (the wife moving to the
husband's home or locality after the marriage) and a system is
followed which not only prohibits marriages from the same agnatic
(male) line but obliges people to marry cognatically (the line being
broken by a female) and whenever possible to marry their own cross-
cousins.[24]   More specifically, both Sinhalese and Tamil marriages
are governed by the following fundamental rules:[25]

Rule 1:   A man should marry his own cross-cousin.
Rule 2:   A man may not marry his parallel-cousin (his sister).
Rule 3:   A man may not marry his paternal grandfather's brother's
          blood daughter (his elder sister).
Rule 4:   A man may not marry his brother-in-law's paternal uncle's
          wife.
Rule 5:   It is not considered improper for a man to marry his
          paternal grandmother's brother's wife's sister's daughter.
Rule 6:   It is not considered improper for a woman to marry her
          stepfather's cousin of the first degree, for although a
          cousin of the first degree of her mother's husband is
          looked upon as an elder or younger brother of her mother,
          there is no impropriety in the marriage.
Rule 7:   It is not improper for a man to marry his maternal aunt's
          granddaughter, provided he is not already married to her
          daughter.

Finally, marriages are endogenous to caste and in both cases they
can be terminated by mutual consent.[26]

The similarities between Tamils and Sinhalese also extend to
matters of inheritance.   The general rule is that property is
inherited through the male line and though divided over all the

sons, the eldest son's share is normally the largest.   Nevertheless,
daughters retain certain rights on the father's property and when
they marry they are given a dowry or presents to comprise their
share.[27]

In terms of their customs the two communities again share much
in common.   These include celebrations or ceremonies associated
with birth, puberty and death, segregation of women during menstruation, the prevalence of arranged marriages, ostracism or
disapproval of inter-caste marriages (though not of extramarital
relations such as concubinage), taboos on the wife referring to her
husband by name and the fact that husband and wife do not eat
together.[28]

Individual features of these kinship systems are characteristic
of many Asian patrilineal societies, but when they are viewed
together they convey an overwhelming impression of deep-rooted
similarity.   In fact they appear to be essentially the same.

As noted earlier, caste is hierarchical in nature and it is
an important factor in the social organisation of Sinhalese villagers
and Tamil labour.   The upper castes had traditionally held positions
of authority in local society and caste tended to be almost synony-
mous with class.   This pattern was structured by a network of
kinship relations and it was this which served to perpetuate the
existing distribution of economic resources, political power and
social control.

The distribution of economic resources was largely determined
by the patrilineal system and the normal mode of inheritance   This
tended to vest control of resources in male members of the family.
Cross-cousin marriages reinforced the concentration of wealth,[29]
and taken together with the high incidence of patrilocality, gave
rise to a system which placed importance on "father-right", on a
patriarchal form of kinship structure and an ideology sustaining
the domination which it implied.[30]

Such a system required control over the production and reproduction activities of women.   There was a clearly defined division
of labour in these societies; women were in charge of the (private)
household activities, while men were in charge of those production
activities which linked the individual household with the rest of
society.   When women were involved in work outside the household,
there was again a strict division of labour.   The ideology

pertaining to these activities always placed them lower than those
of the men, thus stengthening the notion of male authority. Women
were considered to be there to serve the men and both their production
and reproduction activities were under male control.

The ideology underlying the system as a whole placed household
reproduction activities in the field of "natural biological functions",
denying these activities the status of "work". Women's work in the
house was considered a "low" task and even for a low-caste man it
was felt demeaning to wash the dishes or to cook the meals.[31] This
was reinforced by other customs and beliefs which conjured up an
image of women as inferior, unclean, fickle and generally "wrong".[32]

The situation was therefore such that economic resources tended
to be concentrated amongst the most powerful men in their society.
And these men felt that all women were there to serve their needs.
Their own wives were their private property and they were certainly
not to be touched by other men. On the other hand, they considered
themselves as having the right and the power to make use of other
women and control their lives.[33] Even when caste authority began
to be replaced by other forms, female subordination was still maintained. And though Tamil and Sinhalese communities underwent
different changes, the notion of male superiority and control over
women was still retained and constituted a significant part of their
kinship relations.

Inroads into the social background of estate workers

In recent years there are several forces that have begun to
make inroads into this pattern. The first has to do with the
fact that the objective basis of these ties, i.e. the control over
wealth and other resources, is no longer of such validity in the
case of these estate workers. In the case of the Tamils there
was in any case very little property involved. Those who arrived
from India were not at all "well off", and those who managed to
acquire or who had some land "back home" in India had returned there
during the course of the post-independence period when the repatriation issue had come to a head.

In the case of the Sinhalese there existed a double dimension.
Those who worked on the coconut plantations were often people who
had their ties with the villages and who worked on the estates

when there was need for additional labour.   Because of this,
because they were normally in possession of (or in line for) other
resources, the Sinhalese early workers accepted the logic of kinship ties and its implications for inheritance and for property
rights.   Colonial fiscal policy of the nineteenth century
facilitated the concentration of land;   it led to evictions, forced
sales and consequent landlessness, and it was the Sinhalese who were
in this way pauperised who were forced regardless of their predilec-
tions or inclinations to look for work on tea and rubber plantations,
as well as in the more acceptable coconut estates.

For these workers there was little validity in notions relating
to the transfer of property or wealth.   This was further exacerbated
by the fact that massive unemployment had led men to search for jobs
outside the village.   As we have seen, it was the women left behind
who broke away from traditional ties that had served to subordinate
their position vis-à-vis men.

The second force that served to question the traditional
hierarchy was the increase in the level of trade unionisation.
The most important effect of this was to facilitate a shift in the
balance of power to those castes which were now the more numerous.
High caste workers who had hitherto maintained their superior position on the basis of a traditional caste rationale now had to give
way to a new situation where the more numerous low caste groups
suddenly found themselves with far more influence in matters
relating to social and political organisation of the lives of the
workers.   The impact of this on women, however, was (as we shall
see) much more limited.   It is true that women in the lower castes
tended to be far more vocal about their problems than those of the
higher castes and to that extent it would appear that their
grievances would attract more attention.   And yet so far, with few
exceptions, the trade unions have remained male-dominated institutions.   The participation of women is more or less limited to paying
their membership fees and to making their complaints to the thalavar,
their representative.   Because of this there is the tendency to
maintain an ideology of male superiority and its implications.   It
is true that one observes concern amongst a few of the younger generation to be more active in asserting their rights as plantation
workers, but this is still by far the exception rather than the rule.
Most women think that trade union activities are a man's arena, an
area with which they should have little to do.

We have so far considered the implications of and changes in
the social background of the estate labour and we have observed
that the traditional structure implied control of the production and
reproduction activities of women.   These traditions have been
retained for a number of historical reasons, one of the most
important of which was the fact that they served the interests of
those in authority.   With the breakdown of the traditional base of
these relations changes have occurred; these have led to a shift
in the balance of power within estate labour, but the principle of
male superiority has been retained.   In a few cases, where the
breakdown of the family's economic base has completely shaken
traditional ties and where women have had to support their families
by themselves, this has also had the effect of creating a greater
degree of independence for the women involved.

Notes

[1] Census of India (Madras, 1931), No. 5, p. 85.

[2] See A.C. Meyer: Caste and kinship in Central India (London,
Routledge and Kegan Paul, 1966); A. Beteille: Caste, class and
power (Berkeley, University of California Press, 1971); E.R. Leach
(ed.): Aspects of caste in South India, Ceylon and North-West
Pakistan (Cambridge, Cambridge University Press, 1960); J.M. Hutton:
Caste in India (London, Oxford University Press, 1963.)

[3] There has been a considerable amount of occupational mobility
with the spread of commercialisation in the twentieth centry.

[4] The Adi-Dravidas or the Panchamas (literally meaning the
fifth class or outcastes) will for reasons of convenience be referred
to as the lowest caste and not (as they strictly are) as outcastes.

[5] Green in his study on the castes on Sri Lankan estates notes
that the common castes included the Padaiyachis and the Kapu as
the non-Brahmin castes.   Among the Adi-Dravidas or the Panchamas
he notes that there are a great many Pallans, Paraivans and
Chakkiliyans.   (L. Green: The planter's book of caste and custom
(Colombo, the Times of Ceylon Company, Ltd. and London, Blackfriars
House, 1925), Chapter 2).   Jayaraman also looks into the caste issue
on the estates in his three case studies (R. Jayaraman: Caste continuities in Ceylon: A study of the social structure of three tea
plantations (Bombay, Popular Prakashan Press, 1975.)

[6] Hinduism envelopes a complex array of customs and practices.
Central to it are ideas such as samsara (rebirth), the view that an
individual's actions will determine his or her position in their
next life.   The idea of sin (papa) merit (punya), salvation (moksha)
and duty (dharma) are an integral part of the way that they look at
life and relate to people.   And at any level of life or of

reincarnation woman was considered to be inferior to man.   There
was a belief in the minds of these people that a man who failed to
live "a good life" could be reborn a woman.   At its very roots,
therefore, Hinduism valued a woman a lesser being.   If she fulfilled
her duties and led "a good life", she could aspire to becoming a man
in the next life, one step closer to <u>moksha</u> to which all aspired.
See M.N. Srinivas: <u>Religion and society among the Coorgs of South
India</u> (Oxford, Clarendon Press, 1952).

[7] See K.M. de Silva: "Resistance movements in 19th century Sri
Lanka", in M. Roberts (ed): <u>Collective identities, nationalisms and
protest in modern Sri Lanka</u> (Colombo, Marga Institute, 1979) pp. 129-
152.   Also K.T. de Silva: "The demise of Kandyan feudalism", in
Morrison <u>et al</u>: <u>The disintegrating village</u> (Colombo, Lake House
Investments, 1979), pp. 43-70.

[8] Jayaraman had argued that the kangany system has helped to
perpetuate caste and kin groups among the Tamilian estate labourers
in Sri Lanka for each subkangany group was relatively homogenous
in terms of caste and kinship.   In the old estate system, workers
had to align with their subkangany's group and with the one head
kangany and in reality this meant that a large number of the Adi-
Dravidas had to work under Sudra Kanganies (Jayaraman, op.cit.,
pp. 57-64).

[9] Observed in Green, op.cit., and confirmed by interviews with
senior superintendents who said that although lines were not consciously allotted in this way, the head kangany had a say in the
decision and he followed the custom of placing certain castes in
certain concentrations.

[10] The most elaborate celebrations relate to the festivals
of Deepavali, Pongal and Adi Poussai.   Also celebrated are Vael,
Shiva Ratri, the fast of Perumal and St. Anna's Day.

[11] The coming-of-age ceremony of the girl, known as the <u>ruthu
sadangu</u>, is a significant ceremony in the family.   But the con-
finement reinforces the notion that there is something unclean about
a woman during this period.   This feeling is perpetuated by habits
such as not touching the food that is to be served to the rest of
the family at any time when she has her menstruation.   In fact, she
is at these times treated as somebody who could pollute the others
if she came into contact with them.

[12] In a typical Vellalan marriage, the bride has to make a shape
like a net hole with the first fingers of each hand and look towards
the star Arunditi.   This symbolises wifely duty and constancy.   The
rituals also stress the subservient role of the female to the male.

[13] Funeral rites are considered to be very important on the
estate and only men are allowed to partake of the rites involved.

[14] Sanskritisation as mentioned earlier is the historical
process by which castes move to a higher rank in the caste hierarchy.

[15] W.A. Wiswa Warnapala: Civil service administration in Ceylon (Colombo, Department of Cultural Affairs, 1974), p. 8; R. Pieris: Sinhalese social organisation (Colombo, Ceylon University Press, 1956), p. 192. See also V. Samaraweera: "Economic and Social Developments Under the British, 1796-1832", in K.M. de Silva (ed.): University of Ceylon, history of Ceylon (Colombo, University of Ceylon Press Board, 1973), Vol. III, p. 60.

[16] R. Percival: An account of the island of Ceylon (London, 1803), p. 194.

[17] Instances of polyandry have been noted. However, this was not considered an "ideal" situation so much as a solution that was resorted to in "abnormal" circumstances (for example when the man travelled away from the household as a warrior, etc.) and it was not a part of the wider social system.

[18] V. Samaraweera: "Economic and social developments under the British, 1796-1832", in K.M. de Silva, op. cit., pp. 64-65.

[19] M. Roberts, "Elite Formation ...", Collective identities, nationalisms and protest in modern Sri Lanka, op. cit., p. 277.

[20] See N. Sharmugaratnam: "Impact of plantation economy and colonial policy on Sri Lanka peasantry", in Economic and Political Weekly, 17 January 1981; and Report of the Kandyan Peasantry Commission, Sessional Paper XVIII of 1951, passim.

[21] These different levels are called upon for different functions and customs. Day-to-day living involves only the nuclear family; the second level was drawn in for births and puberty rites (and in both communities it was the mother's brother who played the important role); the third level participated in marriage ceremonies, while the last level - the caste or subcaste - would all come together in the case of deaths and the subsequent funeral rites. These patterns are the same in the case of both Sinhalese and Tamils. On this see Jayaraman, op. cit., Chapters 5, 6 and 7; R.H. Pieris, op. cit., chapters on kinship and marriage.

[22] The way in which terms applied to lineal relatives are extended to certain collateral relatives, for example, reveals a distinction between parallel and cross relatives which is true in both cases.

[23] Jayaraman, op.cit., 1975, p. 140; Pieris, op. cit. 1956, p. 219; and G. Obeyesekere: Land tenure in village Ceylon (Cambridge, Cambridge University Press, 1967), p. 37.

[24] Monogamous relations, however, seem on the whole to be part of Roman Dutch law influences in the case of the Sinhalese and it does not seem to have been so strict earlier. (See R. Knox: An historical relation of Ceylon (Glasgow, James MacLehose and Sons, 1911), Chapter VII.

25 These seven rules have been taken from Pieris' study of the early Sinhalese organisation (Pieris, op. cit., pp. 216-219). They have been verified and cross-checked in the course of field interviews with estate workers of both Tamil and Sinhalese origin where it was found that they applied more or less the same rules.

26 For the endogamity of castes see G. Obeyesekere, op. cit., p. 17 and Pieris, op. cit., p. 177. Also see the various case studies of Jayaraman on the Tamil estates and the descriptions therein (Jayaraman, op. cit., studies by Pieris and Jayaraman (p. 200 and p. 188 respectively). This is also observed in the case study by Leach (E.R. Leach: Pul Eliya - a village in Ceylon: A study of land tenure and kinship (Cambridge, Cambridge University Press, 1961), pp. 90-91.

27 Obeyesekere, op. cit., pp. 37-39. Leach, op. cit., p. 74. This was also the pattern observed in the field studies.

28 Jayaraman, op. cit., pp. 170-192; Pieris, op. cit., pp. 174, 216-217 and 224-228. Most of these were also observed in the course of fieldwork.

29 Leach, op. cit., p. 86.

30 In the Sinhalese case, there were two kinds of marriages. There were binna marriages (where a man lives uxorilocally with his wife's father or with her in the case of her father's death; in this case, the wife retained a share of her father's wealth after marriage) and there were diga marriages (where the woman leaves her paternal house and resides virilocally with her husband; in this case, she loses her claims and rights over her father's property after marriage). (Obeyesekere, op. cit., p. 43.) Diga marriages were the general rule (Pieris, op. cit., p. 219.)

31 This is well illustrated by considering the paddy cultivation cycle. (Pieris, op. cit., pp. 78-85.) Here we see that there exists a definite division of labour. The men do the ploughing and the women do the weeding, thinning and transplanting. The reaping is done by one or the other. Pieris indicates that "the women's work is to gather up the corn after the reapers" (ibid. p. 81) while Weerasooria considers a song which is sung of female reapers, "Swinging the golden sickles raised to the sky, stepping down to the fields, the damsels reap the paddy". See N.E. Weerasooria: Ceylon and her people (Lake House, Colombo, 1970), p. 141. The lower status of female labour is indicated by statements like "There is little work to be done until the crop ripens except the women's work of weeding, thinning and transplanting". (Pieris, ibid. p.80). On the other hand, men did not do any work within the household. These tasks were done solely by the women. This was seen as "natural" work for the woman and it was seen more as a function of her biology than as a task itself.

32 An indication of the uncleanliness of the woman was expressed in the attitude of society during her menstruation. "So long as the women have their infirmities or flowers upon them, they are accounted very unclean, in so much that the very house is polluted in that degree that none will approach near it. And even she herself cares not to conceal it, but calls out to them that come near, that they may avoid her house." (Knox, op. cit., 1911, p. 150.)

[33] The right of the high caste man to take a low caste concubine has been noted several times. For this, see W. Sabonadiere: _The coffee planter of Ceylon_ (Colombo, Mees, J.P. Green and Co., 1866), p. 85.

Chapter 4

THE PRODUCTION AND REPRODUCTION ACTIVITIES OF WOMEN

On the contemporary estates women tend to be employed in a few limited and highly specialised occupations, usually tasks requiring a great deal of skill. Some are engaged in weeding, tea sifting, rubber milling or rubber lamination, but they are few in number and by far the majority are concentrated in two main tasks, plucking the tea and tapping the rubber. On coconut estates there is, as we have seen, far less labour required and if women do almost every task except picking the nuts and cutting the contour drains, there are not many involved and numerically these women are of far less importance.

At the same time all women undertake a wide range of household tasks - cooking, cleaning, caring for children and other family members, fetching the water and firewood, and in general, catering to the needs and fancies of their husbands and children. Women do most of the tasks that fall within the ambit of the household unit and serve the reproduction of the family and the labour force.

To undertstand the totality of their working life and the pains and gains that they receive for it, it is necessary to understand the nature of their tasks, the time involved, the benefits that accrue to these estate women and the controls that are placed on them in their situation. The welfare and other facilities are also important dimensions in their existence. And yet even here an appreciation of their concrete situation is only complete when it is seen in the wider context of labour control and labour organisa-tion and of the capitalist nature of almost any plantation system.

The remaining chapters examine this contemporary situation, viewing the lot of women workers in Sri Lankan estates in the light of the earlier historical and social analysis. But first it is important to convey a vivid impression of the nature of their work and of their daily lives. It is important to portray as clearly as possible the drab, empty, futureless existence that so many endure. This chapter is concerned with a description of their day-to-day tasks. Chapter 5 will examine the income, expenditure and indebtedness patterns which frame their lives; Chapter 6 will discuss their various welfare facilities, Chapter 7 the question of trade unionisation and, on the basis of this, a last chapter will outline some tentative suggestions on the possible areas for ameliorative action.

The daily life of the female estate worker

Describing the daily life of a female worker is important for two reasons. Firstly, it provides a necessary factual base, a better understanding of the myriad of tasks and expectations, economic or otherwise, with which she is confronted and of what - after all her labours - is actually accomplished, of what she achieves. And, secondly, it serves to lend an appreciation of the nature of her tasks, of the possibility of her undertaking "non-work" activities, of having free time. Together, it is hoped that these two dimensions will be enough to give at least a feeling for the lot of these women.

In many respects the life of the tea plucker is the most severe. The majority of the women who are employed on Sri Lankan estates are engaged in plucking tea, but nor is the life of the rubber tapper or the coconut worker so very different. They have a very similar existence, though their hours are less. For this reason, and to avoid unnecessary duplication, attention will focus here on the tea plucker's life as an "ideal" case.

In Sri Lanka the official working day for agricultural labour is eight hours, though this can vary in practice according to the nature of the task. This does not normally include the time that is spent in travelling to and from work - it is time on the field. In the case of the estates Sinhalese women often have a very long journey walking to work and for all women workers there are many more hours devoted to other tasks that are not seen as "work" but are nevertheless essential in the reproduction work in the household unit.

The daily life of the tea plucker starts well before sunrise. For the village woman, walking a considerable distance to reach the field this could mean getting up at 3 a.m., while for the resident estate worker, it normally means that she gets up an hour later, at about 4 a.m. These women then have to fetch whatever water the family needs (and in most estates this has to be fetched from a very long distance). They then wash up remaining pots and pans and set about the task of preparing meals (sometimes preparing meals for midday as well). Non-residents have no choice but to make their noon meal and to take it with them as there are no food-stuffs available for them at their place of work and, as in most cases, the distances involved are far too great for them to return and to eat at home.

In any case women serve the morning meal to the men in the
family when they wake up and then to the children.   They then get
their children ready for school and, if they have small children who
are as yet too young to go to school, they still have to prepare some
milk for them.   The women are then in a position to sit and eat
their own meals, they tidy up the line room and send their children
to school.   In the case of non-resident workers it is still too
early to send their children to school when they leave home and this
task has to be left to other family members - generally female, and
usually an older daughter or else the grandmother.   After that the
women leave for work; on the way Tamil women (and sometimes non-
residents) trudge to the crèche and leave their smaller children
with the crèche attendant (if there is a crèche) or with the ayah
whose task it will be to look after them while the women work.   (If
the crèche does not provide free milk, the women leave prepared milk
with the attendant at the same time).   All of this has to be completed before the women report for muster at 7 a.m., or on days when
there is cash plucking available, an hour earlier.[1]

When the woman reports for muster, she is told which field she
will be working in.   If she is late in reporting for work (sometimes
even by as little as a few minutes) she may at times even be sent
away until the following day thereby being denied a full day's wage.
She is simply "chased away" by the field kanganies or the field
officer in charge.   Allowances might be made if the woman is
pregnant, by allowing her to make up for the time that she has lost
at the end of the day, but more generally, this situation creates
an air of anxiety and places a very real pressure on the woman "to
get things done".[2]

Following muster, the woman collects her basket from the muster
shed, and then she walks with the others to her place of work.   This
in itself can take quite a considerable time, the distances involved
on large estates being up to several miles.[3]   When the women start
plucking, crying in unison in Tamil "Poliyo, Poli" ("May these
baskets be soon full"), they pluck the first young leaves and throw
them into their baskets after raising them rather as if in an attitude of worship to the gods.   After this, they pluck the leaves
continuously (the bud and the two tender leaves next to it) until
12 noon.   They do so under the gaze of the field kangany with little
possibility of conversation or light relief and regardless of weather.

At noon the plucker carries her load to the weighing shed where she waits in line until her load for the morning is weighed and after which she is free.   She hurries to collect her children and babies from the crèche (pulekamer) and she returns to the lines. Village women for their part rest a while and eat packed lunches and when necessary feed or suckle children left in the crèche. Tamil women go home to prepare food for the family and to feed their men and their children.   They then eat themselves, often feeding the babies at the same time because of their shortage of time.   If these women have enough time, they wash the dishes, straighten the home in as far as it is needed and set out once again to restart their work.   On the way, they again drop the younger children and babies in at the crèche and report back for work in the field at 1 p.m.[4]

The work of the tea plucker is monotonous and always repetitive and it is carried throughout the day regardless of wind or rain. If the woman commits some irregularity in plucking (such as plucking a hard leaf or picking a stone and putting it into the basket) the kangany (or field officer) is quick to note the fact and in case of repeated faults he "blackguards" the plucker and reprimands her in no uncertain terms for her careless behaviour.   If the matter is taken up with senior officers, she may be sent home but in the majority of such cases she is strictly reprimanded or fined in some way.   The presence of "mature" leaves, if it is detected, would result in punishment for the overseer who overlooked it and, if only for this reason, he (and the overseers are all men), is likely to be as care-ful as he can in his supervision.   In this way the hierarchical and patriarchal nature of estate organisation acts as a very effect-ive means of controlling the women.

On these days when there is a normal or a poor crop to be plucked, work normally stops at 4 p.m.   When there is an abundant crop, the women may in practice pluck for considerably longer, some-times even as late as 5.30 p.m.   After that, they have again to carry their leaves to the weighing shed or some central spot for weighing.   The weight recorded is noted down on their "chits" (small scraps of paper) and on the checkroll, and the women return once again to their homes.   In the case of residents, this would normally be at about 6 p.m. and in the case of the non-resident workers, very much later, women reaching their village homes at about 7 p.m.

The weighing procedure recording the quantity of leaves which
a woman plucks is a point that warrants some degree of elaboration.
Weighing is carried out at least twice a day and what is more, it is
done outside the "working day". In other words, the time which is
required for this is not paid by the estate; it is outside the
eight hours' work that is done on the plucking field. There is a
weighing area (sometimes near the field but very often quite a considerable distance away) to which these women have to carry their
baskets of leaves. If there are three weighings, the first is at
9 a.m., the second at 12 noon and the third at 4 p.m. At the
weighing shed, the women stand in line and time is spent looking
through the leaves, sorting out coarse leaves or twigs which may
have accidentally fallen into the basket. When that is done, the
leaves are then weighed and the weight is noted down by the officer
in charge. One kilogram is normally subtracted for the weight of
the weighing basket and in the rainy season up to two kilograms are
also subtracted for the weight of the moisture that is on the leaves.
The weight that is recorded is then written down on a small slip of
paper (the chit) and this is pinned on the woman's blouse or put into
her basket.

On occasions nursing mothers are allowed one hour off after the
first weighing to feed their babies, but there are still estates
which do not recognise the need for "feeding time". On those that
do the women go back to the crèche if it is nearby (or some older
child arrives with the baby) and the mother sits down by the path
and feeds her child. After that she returns to plucking the leaves.
After the final weighing, the officer in charge collects the various
chits given to the women in the course of the day and notes the total
weight of leaves brought in in a checkroll register.

When these women eventually reach their homes (having collected
their children again on the way), they have little chance of any
respite and must immediately set about their household chores. They
collect the firewood, fetch the water they need and begin their preparation of the evening meal. It is simply assumed that women will
do these tasks. Men and children sometimes help in collecting wood,
but generally, this work is left for the women to do. The women
must bathe the children and change their clothes. If the dhobi
(washerman) does not service them (and it is very often the case that
he does not) the women must also wash the clothes themselves. They
then clean themselves. After that they wash the afternoon dishes

(if they have not been done) and set about preparing the evening
meal.   In the case of non-residents, the pressures involved in
doing all this are even greater because they arrive back at their
homes at a much later hour.

Once the meal is prepared and ready, women serve their husbands
and other men of the household; after that the children have to be
fed, and it is only when that is done that the women have the time
to sit down and to eat their own food.   They then prepare their
children for bed.   In the case of residents, women eventually go to
sleep at about 10 p.m. while in the case of the non-residents it is
often much later.

There is very little difference in any day in the pattern of
the daily life of the female tea plucker.   Whether it is raining
or whether it is not, she has to follow the same routine of work
on all workdays.   The length of the workday might vary a little
with the nature of the crop (when there is a good crop, she might be
working from 6 a.m. to 5.30 p.m. in the field).   But in any case,
in spite of this, she is responsible for her tasks and she has to
undertake all the tasks described above.   Where she fails she is
sent home or she is met with violence.   Hers is a life that is
long, seemingly endless and extremely arduous.   There may exist
exceptions to this pattern, but they are few and they are very far
between.   The pattern of work is such that it invariably tells on
them.   It is a life well captured in the following lines of an old
poem:

Withered roses
their days remembered in thorns
unchanged in each detail:
Days like other days -
So have the hundred years
gone one by one
to the tom-tom throb ....
Eight hours in a day, seven times in a week;
Thus their lifeblood flows, to fashion this land
a paradise for some.

Plantation work in the lives of women workers

Most of the Tamil workforce on Sri Lankan estates have been
carrying out the same tasks for all their lives, many of them for
as long as 40 years.   They started at the age of 10-13 as "child
labour" and although they may have changed estates because of their
marriage, this life was all that they had ever known.   The Sinhalese
were different, if only because they had recently turned to the
estates as a source of employment.   In their lives there was no
history of estate work passed on from mother to daughter, nor was it
necessarily assumed that this was the only work that their children
could eventually have.   Tamil girls knew from the time they were
born that they would be tea pluckers.   It was instilled in them as
children that this was their future, whereas it was individual
deprivation which brought Sinhalese women to consider work on the
estates.   This is particularly true in the case of the tea pluckers,
less so for low-country crops such as rubber and coconuts.   In the
Sinhalese case, the majority of women had not been engaged in paid
labour in the past.

Hard though it may still appear today to an outside observer,
this account reflects quite a considerable improvement in the working situation that many of the Tamil women had experienced in the
past.   This is especially true of the older tea pluckers, many of
who can remember a ten or even an eleven-hour day.   Not surprisingly,
the way these women viewed their own situation varied according to
their age and their circumstances:

    (i)   the old Tamil women said that there had been a definite
          improvement - now the work was less tiring;

   (ii)   young Tamil women who had seen no change said that
          life as a plucker or rubber tapper had always been
          the same; and

 (iii)   for some Sinhalese women, the present situation was a
          definite improvement, because they had been able to
          find no work at all within their own village.

The latter case is perhaps in need of elaboration.   The point here
is that the Sinhalese women worked on the estates for no other
reason than that they were in difficulties; they had no husband
or their husband was unemployed; the latter was not therefore a
preference so much as a need.

Nor did the women who were interviewed (Tamil or Sinhalese)
feel that rewards that the estate was prepared to give them were
sufficient to make it worth while exerting themselves over and
above the basic requirements needed to earn a wage.   For the
Sinhalese, just to have work was itself something they had to be
grateful for.   But for the Tamils, with no other life at all outside the estate, there was very much a felt need for further
incentives.   According to the older women, there had been far more
work for tea pluckers in the past.   Now they certainly earned far
more, at least in cash terms, but they could buy less with it;   they
maintained very firmly that on many estates the picking norm was so
high that few of them could really hope to exceed it, and that if
they did they received no more than 17 cents per kilogram for
"overweight" and 25 cents per kilogram in times of cash plucking.[5]
It was simply not worth the additional effort that they had to apply.
The Sinhalese, however, were pleased with any opportunity to earn
something extra and they were far less critical in this respect.

The attitude of men to the idea of their women working on the
estate is difficult to generalise.   In the case of Sinhalese women,
their menfolk, that is, those who had men (and the majority of
those interviewed in fact did not), were happy that their women had
actually managed to find some sort of work since they themselves
were generally unemployed.   They were unhappy with the fact that
their women were away from the home for so long and for such long
hours;   they grumbled and were continually asking the women to come
back early.

Amongst the Tamils the situation was different.   There was
no sympathy at all with the women's position and no encouragement
of an understanding or a sympathetic nature.   Men insisted that
their women went out to work;   they scolded them if they were not
at work on time;   they demanded that they worked when there was
extra time;   in short, they insisted that they earned the maximum
possible.

Reflections on the nature of these women's tasks

The most striking feature that comes out regarding household
tasks of women on the estate is that they continue to maintain as
far as is physically possible the sexual division of labour that
existed in traditional society and that they do so regardless of

caste, economic status or place of residence. It seems quite
clear that this division of labour is rooted in a traditional value
system or ideology in which the man is primarily responsible for
activities outside the home - for earning the money, doing the
shopping and generally bringing home the means by which the family
members would be able to live. The woman's role lay in the house
and in household tasks. In the context of the estates the context
was different - the women were "working" - but nevertheless, the
old values were still retained with the result that women were
engaged in both tasks.

Several aspects need to be emphasised concerning the full
range of tasks that the woman was forced to do. Firstly, all the
estate women also do household tasks, whether they are tea pluckers,
rubber tappers or casual workers on coconut plantations. The only
variation is in the amount of time devoted to various activities
and this is dictated largely by the demands of their estate work.
Secondly, the monotony and repetition of their tasks needs to be
emphasised. Thirdly, the fact that their tasks recur at regular
intervals throughout the day underlines the unending nature of their
work and impresses on them the fact that it is never over. Fourthly,
these tasks take up so much of the day that they have little or no
time left for social contacts outside their work and their household even if their husbands allowed them to have them. This limited
their perspectives to their immediate surroundings. Finally, all
of these features together tended to place these women in a position
where they were always working, egged on and controlled by men from
the time they wake up to the time that they went to bed (and still
beyond that). This was a pattern of life in considerable contrast
to that of men. Men were dominant, and if the women cooked badly,
were late for work, or were found irritating, they were often
subjected to violence and to abuse.

In this situation, one can readily understand the pressure
that is put on the children and especially the girls, to take over
some of this burden of work from the mother. This is illustrated
by the fact that when they were asked whether they worked more or
worked less now than they had in the past, most women replied that
when they were unmarried they had been compelled (or felt compelled)
to do more to help out their mother. Once they were married and
had daughters who helped in the housework, things had become a
little easier for them. This was substantiated by unmarried women

who said that they were doing a large amount of household work, and that they had been doing so since they were 9 or 10 years old. What is more, this practice was not a recent innovation; all the very old women who were interviewed firmly maintained that this pattern had existed for as long as they could remember. Perhaps it was only in this way that such women had managed to keep going for so many years.

Indeed, there was a general unanimity regarding the tasks that men ever did in the house. All women said that men did the shopping and sometimes helped them collecting wood for the fire, but they would not do any chores within the house. This was women's work and this was demeaning. In the case of a few of the resident workers and most non-resident women, their menfolk came to their aid in the case of an emergency when they would help in looking after the children and in the cooking. This, however, was usually only the case amongst those who had married of their own free will, and who had often done so against the wishes of their parents.

When they were asked if they did any other work than estate work and the work in the household, there was understandably enough a clear distinction between resident and non-resident women.

Non-residents said that if work was available for them in the village, they would always do that instead of coming to the estate. In point of fact these women frequently worked as casual labour in paddy fields during the peak seasons. This tendency was more marked in the coconut and rubber areas, where labour requirements on the estates were considerably lower. On the other hand, population densities in these low-country areas also meant that it was more difficult for them to find village work.

Among those who were resident on the estate, work outside in the village was not easily available and in most cases (especially tea pluckers) it was practically impossible. Those who had been allocated line rooms were often reticent about outside work in the (often realistic) belief that this might lead to them losing their accommodation. Nevertheless, some of these households were able to take up kitchen gardening and to keep cows.

The basic factor that in practice served to rationalise the double, or multiple, workload of women was, when all is said and done, the attitude of the estate management and of society in general to household tasks. Firstly, they were not considered to be "work" but "natural" tasks for a woman. They were taken for granted, and no thought was given to the extra burden that is being imposed when she worked in the field. Secondly, when the household was faced

with an economic crisis, it was generally the woman who was forced to
bear the brunt of it, because it was her work in the household that
subsidised the fall in income up to a point.   Finally, because the
man and the children were generally given priority, and generally
secured the most and the better food, the woman's general health
and nutritional standards deteriorated first.   The additional
strain and effort on her part went largely unseen because the entire
social and economic system viewed the household sector as something
that was essentially "non-work".   It is to be hoped that the present
description of the workload of estate women has served to show the
limitations and fallacies of such an approach.

The nature and intensity of household work tends to be such
that it places the woman in a well defined, limited and highly
controlled situation.   The estate woman finds that she is always
working, and that additional tasks are readily placed on her within
the home because she is confronted with an ideology that is widely
accepted and which fails to recognise the household chores as "work".
This is therefore another illustration of the way in which women are
marginalised in the estate community.

Notes

[1] It has been noted that muster during the British rule was
often at 5 a.m. (Address of the President to the Directors and
and Planters of the Janatha Estates Development Board and Sri Lanka
State Plantations Corporation, Colombo, 5 July 1980).

[2] Some superintendents realise that in times of labour
shortage, it is useful not to be so strict with the time of arrival
for early morning muster.   In this case, they are prepared to allow
up to 10 minutes tardiness, which is made up by making the woman
work later after the normal hours of work.

[3] On one estate that I visited the superintendent told us that
it took three hours to reach one area in the hills that had to be
plucked.   Clearly, this was an extreme case.

[4] The strain of completing so many activities in this short
time often leads to the neglect of some of them.   In this sense
this is an "idealised" account.   The entire account is of course
for days when work is available.   (See pp. 95-97)-

[5] The term "overweight" refers to the weight of tea plucked
(or rubber tapped) over and above a "norm" which is set for the women
to achieve in any one day.   Cash plucking is a period in which the
women are paid per kilogram with no norms applying;   this generally
refers to additional work over and above their eight hours and it
is employed in order to bring in the full crop during the peak months.

Chapter 5

INCOME, EXPENDITURE AND INDEBTEDNESS

What a woman worker obtains for her labours is very largely a function of income, expenditure and indebtedness, and of the inter-relations that exist between the three. Clearly she does receive somewhat more than this, both in the long term in the form of her pension rights and more immediately by way of indirect wages through the provision of housing, social and welfare services. This chapter however is confined to analysing the real income that the female worker receives regularly and as such excludes long-term benefits and subsidies. As such it is important to take into account not only the money wage that she receives (and that of her family), but also the pattern of expenditure and indebtedness they incur.

These three parameters define to a large extent the immediate returns on the labour that the women worker puts into estate pro-duction and they together determine her standard of living. It is also highly influenced by her role in the family, and whether or not she is a resident on the estate. The situation can in many ways therefore be an intricate one and one that is analytically difficult to confine under normal categories of economic analysis without losing some of the important interconnections that exist. For that reason, this chapter will not aim so much at providing a statistically perfect indexing of income, expenditure and indebted-ness as at bringing out the different social and economic forces that provide the dynamics of these parameters.

These parameters will first be analysed separately and will then be considered together. Throughout, particular attention will be paid to the way in which traditional norms and needs of the estate system serve to reinforce the superiority and control of the man.

Income

The income of a female worker even in money terms is frequently comprised of at least two components: firstly, there is the wage that she receives from the estate, and secondly - in those cases where the opportunity exists - there is the income to be obtained from "additional" work.[1] In by far the majority of situations,it is estate work that yields the major part of her total income, with extra work essentially supplementary in nature. However, there are considerable variations in this pattern from area to area, and both of these sources have therefore to be considered.

It is also important to bear in mind again that the woman is not only a worker but a member of a household, and that her situation and the returns which she herself sees for her various labours are in practice very much influenced by this fact. For this reason the analysis must take account of household income (and later household expenditure and household debts) because these are also in a very real sense determinants of what she eventually receives.

Estate income

Wages on tea, rubber and coconut plantations are neither haphazard nor disorganised, nor are there variations from estate to estate or from one area or one part of the country to another. On the contrary, they are standardised and highly structured; what is more they are governed by a Wages Board to which the Government appoints members and on which trade unions and employers are represented, and whose task it has been to establish the minimum wage since 1944.[2] To this basic wage there are added a number of allowances which are designed to compensate the worker for losses suffered through the increased cost of living. The level and composition of minimum wages for estate workers as of September 1980 is presented in Table 1.

However, even contained in this legally stated minimum wage there are a number of inequalities, most of which tend to work to the disadvantage of women. Firstly, the minimum wage rate for men and women is different, even when they are engaged in exactly the same task at the same or even higher productivity levels. The wages of women are some 25 per cent lower than those of men. Secondly the supplements are based on a cost-of-living index which is supposed to account for the changing costs of the estate worker. However, this index does not reflect the expenditure pattern of estate labour as the main items of their diet are inadequately represented. The minimum wage is multiplied by this index, and since men have a larger initial wage, the supplement which they receive is consequently larger.

Table 1: Minimum wages in the plantation sector (in Rs.)

1 (a)	Tea growing and manufacturing trade	Male	Female	Child
	Basic wage	2.51	2.32	2.07
	Special allowance	3.52	2.44	2.37
	PWASA	0.18	0.12	0.12
	PSAA (10 per cent of the January 1975 rate)	0.50	0.38	0.34
+	TEW wage supplement	0.30	.30	0.30
	Sub total	7.01	5.56	5.20
xx	PSSA (20 per cent of above total including 20 per cent of -/60 ct. reduced from December 1978 wage supplement)	1.52	1.23	1.16
	Sub total	8.53	6.79	6.36
xxx	6 per cent of above total including 6 per cent of -/60 ct. reduced from December 1978 wage supplement	0.55	0.44	0.42
	Sub total	9.08	7.23	6.78
++	25 per cent of the above total including 25 per cent of -/60 ct. reduced from December 1978 wage supplement	2.42	1.96	1.85
	Supplementary allowance as of 1 September 1979	2.50	2.50	2.50
	TOTAL MINIMUM WAGES	14.00	11.69	11.13

1 (b)	Rubber growing and manufacturing trade	Male	Female	Child
	Basic wage	2.65	2.55	2.30
	Special allowance = IDA	3.52	2.44	2.37
	PWASA	0.18	0.12	0.12
x	PSAA (10 per cent of January 1975 rate)	0.59	0.47	0.43
	Price wage supplement	2.65	2.65	2.65
	Sub total	9.59	8.23	7.87
xx	PSSA (20 per cent of the above total as of December 1975)	1.92	1.65	1.57
	Sub total	11.51	9.88	9.44
xxx	6 per cent wage increase (on the above total)	0.69	0.59	0.57
	Sub total	12.20	10.47	10.01
++	25 per cent of the above total	3.05	2.62	2.50
	Supplementary allowance as of 1 September 1979	2.50	2.50	2.50
	TOTAL MINIMUM WAGES	17.75	15.59	15.01

1 (c)	Coconut growing trade	Male	Female	Child
	Basic wage	2.66	2.46	2.21
	Special allowance	3.52	2.44	2.37
	PWASA	0.18	0.12	0.12
	PSAA (10 per cent of January 1975 rate)	0.51	0.38	0.34
	Sub total	6.87	5.40	5.04
xx	PSSA (20 per cent of the above total as of December 1978)	1.37	1.08	1.01
	Sub total	8.24	6.48	6.05
xxx	6 per cent wage increase (on the above total)	0.49	0.39	0.36
	Sub total	8.73	6.87	6.41
++	Plus 25 per cent of above total	2.18	1.72	1.60
	Supplementary allowance as of 1 September 1979	2.50	2.50	2.50
	TOTAL MINIMUM WAGES	13.41	11.09	10.51

Note to Table 1:

The additional allowance of Rs. 3/- per day to daily paid coconut, cocoa, cardamon and pepper growing and manufacturing trade
workers is not to be taken into account for computation of provident
fund, overtime, holiday pay, maternity benefits, etc., and the
allowance will remain at Rs. 2/- per day for work on weekly holidays
as well.

+ Not applicable on estates of less than 100 acres in extent.
x Subject to a maximum of Rs. 25/- per month.
xx Subject to a maximum of Rs. 50/- per month.
xxx Subject to a maximum of Rs. 15/- per month.
++ Subject to a maximum of Rs. 50/- per month.

The result is an increase in the absolute differentials between
men and women. Furthermore, Helen Abell has argued that in cases
where the head of the household is a widow and there is no male
wage earner (and this is the case with the majority of non-resident
labour) increasing differentials place greater financial strains
upon these families in periods of rapidly rising living costs.[3]

Thirdly, although the minimum daily wage is fixed, estate labourers are only paid once a month and what they receive depends on the number of days' work that are actually offered. This varies according to the crop, the area, the season and the yield of the particular estate on which she works. Prior to nationalisation the Permanent Secretary of the Ministry of Plantation Industries stated that 40-50 per cent of the estates could offer work for no more than three days a week; 40 per cent could only offer four days work and only 10 per cent were in a position to offer five days or more.[4] Similar variations are recorded in the Tea Master Plan. The average number of days' work offered in April 1978 varied from 16.4 to 21.9 in four high elevation estates, 17.0 to 19.3 in five mid-elevation estates, and 13.2 to 15.5 in three low-elevation estates.[5]

Similar variations were observed in the course of field studies and these statistics are repeated here in order to emphasise the fact that even though there is a legally stipulated minimum wage, because of the structure of wages, the variation in income can still be large. What is more, in any given locality, it tends to affect women more than men.

For example, using the data for up-country estates in April 1978 calculation reveals that because of the variation that occurred in the number of days worked, there was a difference in income amongst female workers of 34 per cent, the corresponding figure for men being 13 per cent; for low-country estates the figures were 17 per cent amongst women and 12 per cent amongst men, while the difference between the highest up-country and lowest low-country incomes was a remarkable 66 per cent in both of their cases.[6] These are obviously very considerable variations, and they are often particularly bad in the case of women.

The worst repercussions of this are said to have been ameliorated by a law passed in March 1974 legally binding the estates to pay 108 days' work to its registered labour every six months. However, this work has to be averaged over the whole half year; the law does not mean that 18 days' work has to be guaranteed in a particular month, and in the absence of savings this places a great many workers under financial stress in the lean months of the year. In coconut plantations registered labour could not be offered sufficient work during much of 1980 because of the drought.[7] This was apparent throughout most of the region from field observations.

When this was so, and incomes were low, it was particularly
hard for a woman to make up for the loss because there were fewer
alternative sources of employment open to her.   This is confirmed
by the difficulties of casual labourers to whom the legal requirement does not apply.   A large proportion of the casual labour is
female on all estates, and it is they who bear the brunt of any
shortfall in work and who because of the high rate of unemployment
in the villages remain without any income for long periods of time.

Finally, when all is said and done, the division of work on
tea estates where the vast majority of these women are working is
often such that - given the structure of wages and the nature of
the task - women work for much longer hours than men and yet still
earn less.   This is particularly marked in the case of tea estates
which are very labour intensive.   In the case of rubber and coconut estates there is a similar situation in that differences in
earnings also reflect the division of work.   Men tend to be given
those tasks which have a higher earning potential, thus creating
a situation where women are basically seen as cheap labour and
concentrated in time-consuming and labour-intensive activities.[8]
The basic statistics on this can be found in Table 2.   This information only goes up to September 1976, but statistics compiled in
course of field observations reflect just the same pattern.[9]

Women are also far from being compensated proportionately for
any extra efforts which they make in trying to make up for a shortfall in monthly income.   For example, tea pluckers are required
to pick a daily norm of so many kilograms;   if the daily minimum
rate is divided by this norm it can then be expressed as a rate
per kilogram plucked.   When women bring in more than this norm
they are paid for "overkilos" at a basic rate of Rs. 0.17 per kilogram, though this is raised to Rs. 0.25 if they "turn out" for more
than 80 per cent of the days on which work is offered.   The point
in this, however, is that in general the rate per overkilo works
out to be 30-40 per cent lower than the rate per kilogram during
the normal day.[10]

More then that, women pluckers receive a declining rate of
return for each additional kilogram they bring in over the norm.
In other words women who are struggling for additional income
through greater effort are not only paid for this at a lower rate,
but at a rate that becomes lower and lower the more work they put in.

Table 2: Monthly earnings and hours worked

Trade	Category	March 1971		September 1971		March 1972		September 1972	
		Average No. of hours worked/ month	Average earnings per month Rs c.	Average No. of hours worked/ month	Average earnings per month Rs c.	Average No. of hours worked/ month	Average earnings per month Rs c.	Average No. of hours worked/ month	Average earnings per month Rs c.
1. Tea growing and manufacturing	Males	158.97	67.61	142.28	61.75	117.58	70.90	131.10	57.98
	Females	164.39	59.39	150.42	74.70	119.12	49.30	134.75	46.91
	Children								
	Males	127.88	36.51	107.58	43.18	145.73	40.89	119.36	44.06
	Females	153.85	51.41	144.93	42.70	114.36	31.02	109.26	47.34
2. Rubber growing and manufacturing	Males	170.49	73.58	120.46	54.93	158.73	71.48	118.20	55.70
	Females	163.41	58.51	110.12	40.07	148.05	53.84	107.92	39.80
	Children								
	Males	191.38	55.97	103.66	29.76	138.90	41.71	124.50	37.21
	Females								
	Kangan- nies	190.03	100.83	165.48	94.03	--	--	--	--
3. Coconut growing	Males	168.83	74.06	146.59	63.80	63.80	74.66	152.31	69.23
	Females	141.01	46.74	122.98	39.19	131.66	45.47	136.67	43.66
	Children								
	Males	--	--	--	--	152.93	52.48	124.51	36.69
	Females	159.35	45.67	140.32	39.09	--	--	--	--

Table 2 contd....

Trade	Category	March 1972 Average No. of hours worked/ month	March 1972 Average earnings per month Rs c.	September 1973 Average No. of hours worked/ month	September 1973 Average earnings per month Rs c.	March 1974 Average No. of hours worked/ month	March 1974 Average earnings per month Rs c.	September 1974 Average No. of hours worked/ month	September 1974 Average earnings per month Rs c.
1. Tea growing and manufacturing	Males	135.31	66.38	123.21	68.82	118.75	69.84	136.31	87.26
	Females	138.13	53.31	133.47	67.91	138.88	64.57	136.17	66.75
	Children								
	Males	106.62	32.77	130.29	41.65	138.44	54.78	88.09	37.50
	Females	106.19	33.27	147.17	48.21	136.68	52.29	100.12	40.67
2. Rubber growing and manufacturing	Males	150.30	79.39	155.36	97.03	170.47	124.24	116.72	90.28
	Females	132.36	58.86	136.40	69.35	154.56	91.30	102.28	64.67
	Children								
	Males	112.00	40.00	129.71	52.43	131.33	65.00	46.29	28.59
	Females								
	Kanga-nies	--	--	--	--	--	--	--	--
3. Coconut growing	Males	151.02	73.70	144.02	71.88	146.01	85.23	163.97	99.06
	Females	149.00	55.05	125.49	49.52	126.99	59.45	124.29	63.60
	Children								
	Males	146.44	48.24	137.94	47.44	121.18	46.64	133.71	53.92
	Females								

Table 2 cont. ....

Trade	Category	March 1975		September 1975		March 1976		September 1976	
		Average No. of hours worked/ month	Average earnings per month Rs c.	Average No. of hours worked/ month	Average earnings per month Rs c.	Average No. of hours worked/ month	Average earnings per month Rs c.	Average No. of hours worked/ month	Average earnings per month Rs c.
1. Tea growing and manufacturing	Males	152.98	144.21	146.98	133.71	131.00	103.85	143.07	125.00
	Females	162.10	94.79	130.35	79.20	125.92	77.09	139.04	93.44
	Children								
	Males	175.25	69.23	128.63	57.44	81.08	40.27	159.48	62.66
	Females	136.41	65.19	115.56	57.09	89.88	46.88	131.86	60.47
2. Rubber growing and manufacturing	Males	165.82	132.89	142.91	145.74	174.35	175.49	167.30	211.22
	Females	147.73	94.77	130.48	105.19	145.58	127.69	152.18	156.64
	Children	160.50	88.00	122.67	69.67	78.00	60.00	174.00	108.00
3. Coconut growing	Males	145.60	104.23	145.41	108.54	160.79	125.39	158.99	134.26
	Females	135.93	68.22	143.60	76.99	147.45	83.80	126.24	77.53
	Children								
	Males	142.04	64.81	127.15	57.66	130.00	75.00	131.75	75.00
	Females								

Source: Department of Census Statistics - Ministry of Plan Implementation Statistical Abstract of the Democratic Socialist Republic of Sri Lanka - 1977. (Department of Government Printing, Sri Lanka, 1979)

What is more, the rate of decline in the payment for extra work is faster in the lean months when the crop has a low norm. Those months in which they have difficulty in reaching the norm are also those in which the payment per additional kilogram is falling fastest. In these months they have to work harder to reach the basic norm; it is harder for them to pluck any overkilos, and if they do the rate of payment will decline more sharply. In short, women who are forced to work for additional income are being exploited more.[11]

A similar pattern can also be seen on rubber estates. The rubber tapper is allocated a plot of some 200 trees to tap and for that area she is given a standard norm of so many kilograms of latex to collect. She is then paid for overkilos above this norm, the rate varying quite significantly according to the frequency at which she has turned out for work.[12] However, when her income is again translated into rates per kilogram the same declining rate of return and a faster decline in the leaner months can be observed.[13] The situation of these women is basically the same as in the case of tea.

Finally, with regard to the coconut industry, wages and earnings of female workers are somewhat different because a large proportion of the women engaged are casual workers. The main point here is firstly, the fact that they do not have even the minimum statutory level of wages and employment that must be offered and, secondly, that for this reason they do not qualify for the various benefits accruing to registered labour. For example, women are frequently employed in hacking fibre; the normal rate is Rs. 6.50 per cwt. of finished fibre; many of them work until as late as 10 p.m. to earn as little as Rs. 6.50 per day, which is well below the statutory minimum wage.[14] These women do not have assured employment; they are not entitled to the Employers Provident Fund (EFP), maternity benefits, holiday pay, advances of the supplementary increments paid to the others. Some managers have in practice given them many of these benefits, but it is not legally stipulated that they have to do so, and in practice whether they are given it or not depends on the decision of the individual superintendent.

"Non-estate" income and household income[15]

In situations where a woman is faced with financial difficulties, alternative sources of income are obviously important. However, if only because of her pattern of work on the estate and within the household, the opportunities that are in practice open to her are

generally limited. Additional earnings by male members of the family
over and above their normal estate tasks, contribute to household
income from which she is also likely to benefit. For this reason
non-estate income and household income are considered together.

The sources of non-estate income that exist for the workers on
an estate are narrowly circumscribed; they vary quite considerably
from region to region and from estate to estate. The principal
avenues open to them are vegetable cultivation on kitchen gardens
or allotments, cattle (and occasionally other animal) rearing, and
work in the villages. Each of these various sources will be examined
in turn.

Vegetable cultivation, for example, can take two forms. First
of all there is household subsistence production to augment their
income. Small plots are provided on almost all plantations (usually
in the form of kitchen gardens), although in practice these cannot
always be used for reasons of soil or reasons of climate and because
of the prevalent problems with water supplies. Production of this
kind becomes particularly important in periods of economic crises
such as those culminating in the food shortages of the early 1970s.
In this context even small gardens provide a cushioning effect in
times of need; however, in practice they are rarely sufficient to
meet the whole of the household's requirements, and it is not uncommon to find that the plots are even untended.

Secondly, there is also the cultivation of vegetables as a cash-
crop, often on separate allotment areas. This, however is restricted
to small, particularly favourable ecological areas and in practice
almost entirely confined to the Nuwara Eliya/Maskeliya/Hatton
parts of the up-country area. There, favourable climatic conditions
make vegetable production a lucrative business. Interested middlemen come from as far away as Colombo, and it is not uncommon for
them to have regular contracts or agreements with local producers.
The worker (cum producer) is often paid in advance for the crop she/
he produces on a particular plot, and when it is ready the middleman
will come to collect it from the field. The main crops involved
are leeks, potatoes and cabbages, although several other vegetables
are also produced.

It is difficult to assess the importance of cash-crop production
from statistics available as these refer only to an area that is
actually under cultivation and vegetable production is highly intensive in nature.[16] What is clear is that it is particularly important

in small pockets and that families that are seriously involved in
this vegetable production can earn between Rs. 450 and Rs. 600 a month.
This is a conservative estimate, and particular families are known
to earn considerably more.   Furthermore, prices for this garden
produce tend to increase in line with the cost of living.

If only because the woman's working day is normally much longer,
it is the men who are mainly responsible for the plots.   Women are
sometimes involved in fetching water and watering crops, and in some
areas where production is particularly profitable women worked on
the vegetable plots instead of the estates.[17] In a few exceptional
cases this went as far as to create a serious labour problem for
the plantation management.   In areas where a labour deficit already
existed this only served to exacerbate the existing problem and the
management tried to find ways of discouraging "non-estate" work.

Cattle rearing for milk is still in its infancy as a commercial
proposition.   It has recently been pushed very hard by the Minister
of Rural Industrial Development (Mr. Thondaman) who is also President
of the Ceylon Workers Congress and a Member of Parliament from the
Nuwara Eliya/Maskeliya area.   The People's Bank and the Bank of
Ceylon offer loans to estate workers to purchase cattle given the
guarantee and support of the superintendent, and this is granted in
the vast majority of cases.[18] It is estimated that each cow provides
a net income of some Rs. 300 to Rs. 400 a month during the lactation
period.

In many cases superintendents play an active role in organising
the collection of milk by the Milk Board, and in some cases they are
trying to organise workers into co-operatives.[19] However, there are
still many instances where middlemen or licensed agents collect in
a lorry, where the measuring and payment for milk is not standardised
and where marketing works to the disadvantage of the estate worker.
Tending the cattle is essentially a man's responsibility.   It is
still too early to evaluate this programme or to assess the possibility of it creating any significant improvement in the income situation of estate workers.

In those cases where the estates are located near to a village,
a very small proportion of estate men manage to do temporary agricultural work during periods of labour demand.[20] This, we have seen
can comprise an important source of income for non-resident women,
and it is one they prefer.   During these periods wages are considerably higher than those on estates, for a man reaching as high as
Rs. 20-25 per day and for a woman less.

Finally, there are instances where estate workers are engaged
in poultry production, arrack sales, moneylending and petty trading.
Although these may in some cases be lucrative sidelines, they are
so few and far between that they have not been considered in the
analysis of average income patterns.

Turning now to household income, the situation becomes even
more complex for at least three reasons.   Firstly, because multi-
plying the number of working members by the average income does not
give an accurate picture of their estate earnings.   Secondly, because
subsistence "incomes" vary considerably from family to family and
from area to area.   And, thirdly, because it is only a very small
proportion of households which earn "non-estate" incomes.

A sample from one estate in June 1980 revealed that the range
in estate incomes for a household was from Rs. 225 to Rs. 1,311.[21]
The number of workers and the number of days' work were obviously
important in determining a particular household's estate income,
but there was also an inter-relationship between the two.   For
example, the typical estate income for a household with two working
members was found to range from Rs. 225 to Rs. 780.   For a household with three, four or five members the range was between Rs. 996
and Rs. 1,311.[22]   Incomes for larger families overlapped and were
often more or less equal.   In other words, beyond a certain point
household income was not proportional to the number of workers.
There was a cut-off point at about Rs. 1,200-1,300.   What was happening was that once this level of incomes was obtained the total
number of days worked tended to decline.   Furthermore, an analysis
of this trend revealed the interesting fact that it was the male
members who were the first to work less on the estate.   In many
cases the woman continued to work as many days as before.

Another interesting correlation that has been established is
the inverse relationship between the ratio of workers to dependents
on the one hand and the number of days worked on the other.   What
lay behind this was that a couple with young children were forced
to work hard, and once the children were old enough to join their
parents on the estate the number of days' work per household member
began to decrease.   The more workers there were relative to dependents, the faster the fall-off in the number of working days, thus
creating the observed cut-off in household incomes.   However, it
was not an equal reduction in working days for all family members;
it was primarily for the men.

It may well have been that in some cases the men used the time
that they gained for other income-generating activities. However,
this was very limited, and it cannot be said to provide a real explanation of this decline. It is more likely that when the man collected
the family's estate income and found that it was getting larger,
he felt that there was less need for him to work, and that he then
worked less.

With regard to subsistence "incomes", examination of the household budgets of individual families would seem to suggest that a
monetary estimate of Rs. 40.45 per month as the value of produce
grown on kitchen gardens is not unreasonable. Not all families
have or make use of this facility. As we have seen, incomes from
vegetable cultivation and cattle rearing range from Rs. 450-600 and
Rs. 300-400 a month. Again, not all families are engaged in these
activities, and those that are will experience variations in income
from month to month.[23]

As a result it is difficult to provide an accurate estimate of
household income and any one figure would be unreliable. For this
reason it seems safer to speak of ranges of income, and the following
table provides ranges for families of different size.

Table 3: Estimated ranges of household incomes
for families of different size and by
type of activity

No. of workers	E	E+S	E+C	E+C+S	E+V	E+V+S
2	225	265	525	565	675	715
	780	820	1 080	1 120	1 280	1 320
4	966	1 006	1 266	1 306	1 416	1 456
	1 311	1 351	1 611	1 651	1 761	1 801

E = total estate earnings
S = subsistence income
C = income from cattle
V = income from vegetable cultivation

Source: This is based on information collected from the sample of
estates covered in field research.

These figures are considered representative for an average month
on tea and rubber estates (which anyway comprise the vast majority
of female workers).[24] Because of the monthly variation in non-
estate incomes, the lower estimate has been applied in each case.

In short, the table shows a range of incomes for two worker households from Rs. 225 to Rs. 1,320, and for four worker households from Rs. 966 to Rs. 1,801. In both cases the mode will clearly be towards the lower end of the scale according to our sample.

In the case of coconut plantations wages generally tend to be lower, if only because of the fact that there is less work available and because much of it is undertaken on a casual basis. Much of it, as we have said, is on a piece work arrangement. The main alternative open to these people is to work as hired labour on paddy and other agricultural crops. This is highly seasonal, and though wages may be higher than those in the coconut industry (in the range of Rs. 15-20 a day) work of this kind is not always available. Given the high rate of unemployment in most of the villages, this would seem to suggest that workers on coconut estates are amongst the poorest in terms of their household incomes.

Turning to non-resident workers, estate incomes per person are on a par with those of the resident labour when they are working. However, their turnout rates are generally less, they come to work for less days even when it is available on the estates. This seems to suggest that the ratio of estate to non-estate income is different and that they can obtain better paid village work for part of the item. Moreover, subsistence "incomes" are generally higher with a wider range of products on their homestead plots. On the other hand, when it comes to household incomes, the fact that these women are often the only bread-winners within the family makes a big difference. Some of the other members may find casual employment in the village, but it rarely accounts for more than Rs. 100 a month.

Expenditure

When examining the expenditure patterns of estate workers in Sri Lanka there are two crucial features that have to be considered: the mechanics of control with regard to expenditure, and the implications of the actual expenditure pattern for the average woman. Each of these two points will be examined in turn.

The mechanics of control over expenditure

Concerning the first of these features, the control of expenditure, three facts stand out as of major importance. Firstly, on Sri Lankan estates it is almost always the man who on pay day collects

the wages of all family members. In our sample this was found to
be true for over 90 per cent of the resident labour force, and the
main reason that was given by way of an explanation was the fact
that women either worked too late or too far away on the estate to
go to the paydesk or had work that had to be done in the household
sphere. Men in contrast finished earlier and had much more time
to go and collect the pay. In the case of Tamil workers the only
exceptions to this were those in which a working daughter was told
to collect the wages because the father was tired, or (on a few
estates) where the superintendent, confronted with disputes or other
problems relating to pay, had made it a rule that every worker collect
his or her own money. Even in these cases, however, it was
generally true that the money collected was handed over to the eldest
male of the household.

The attitude that was reflected in this situation was also underlying the second point, namely that at no time was this "family"
money given to the woman to run the household or to meet her own
needs. The rigid division of labour in domestic activities was
such that it was the man who was responsible for doing the shopping.
The result was that it was considered "natural" or automatic that
household income should remain in the hands of men. If something
was needed for the house or if the woman wanted some item or other
for herself, she had to ask the man for it, and it was up to the
man to buy what she wanted if he saw fit.

Thirdly, there is no indication to suggest that the woman has
any real say in the way that her income is spent. On the contrary,
it is a well known phenomenon on Sri Lankan estates that there are
fights on pay day when the man takes the household income and spends
it on liquor. The most frequently cited cause for domestic fights
and domestic squabbles is the woman's objection to her hard-earned
income being squandered on drink.

In this way the different working hours of men and women that
characterise the daily pattern of life on tea estates and the division of labour existing within the household, together with the
underlying social values that justified them, served to reinforce
male domination through the control of household income and of the
way it was spent. As such it fits the general ethos and ideology
of these communities.

And yet it is also instructive to study those exceptional cases
in which this general pattern does not apply. Together these bring
out the point that when women, by force of circumstances, are non-
conformist and are forced to live outside the generally accepted
behaviour patterns of their community, this also leads to a change
in the way that income and expenditure are controlled and in the
proportion devoted to individual items.

Three such cases or circumstances can be clearly identified
normally associated with periods of economic or social crisis for
the people concerned. The largest such group are the non-resident
workers on the tea and rubber estates who rarely have menfolk working
on the estate, and who have no option but to collect their pay themselves. As we have seen, their economic circumstances are frequently
such that they are the sole wage earners in the family, their men
either being unemployed or away seeking employment in other areas.
They tend (as we have seen) to belong to the lowest social level in
the village, and the fact that they live more freely with men and
have children outside marriage also places them outside traditional
norms and accepted patterns of village behaviour. With responsibility for looking after the needs of the entire household resting
upon their shoulders, these women keep the money they earn; they
decide how the money is spent, and this pattern is even continued
when the men are there.

The second group who do not conform to the more general pattern
are those who have taken independent decisions about their marriage.
It was not uncommon for those women who have had "love" marriages
(as against arranged marriages, which was the case with the majority)
to be ostracised from the family for a period of time.[25] These women,
however, were on the whole much freer with their husbands. They
had a greater role and say in the way their incomes were spent, and
even if the husband had the final say in matters of shopping, they
were in a much better position to make their opinions felt.

Thirdly, the position of a particular family in the caste hierarchy also had an influence of the woman's ability to determine
expenditure patterns. Low caste women seemed more forthright in
their demands than those from the higher castes for reasons which
have been given in earlier chapters.[26] Though it remained the case
that men generally collected the money and that the men spent it,
lower caste women were able to assert a far greater influence on

patterns of expenditure. They voiced their opinions with greater
force and they had considerably more say in the way that incomes
were spent.

In short, in each of these three cases in which the woman had
more say, she came in one sense or another from a marginalised group,
and from one that was somewhat outside the accepted norms of her
community.

The actual expenditure pattern and its implications

The second feature that has to be examined as a part of this
theme is the actual expenditure pattern of these estate families.
In this respect it is important to show how the household's income
is in practice spent, the relative share devoted to particular items,
and what the woman eventually receives in exchange for her efforts.
Though there is obviously a considerable amount of variation in this
from family to family, there are nevertheless certain basic features
that they have in common.

On most estates, for example, a certain proportion of the household's staple foods are supplied "on advance" from the estate management, the corresponding sum being deducted from the worker's wages
at the end of the month.[27] The amount that they can obtain depends
very much on the number of people that there are in the household,
but in almost all cases they can obtain a certain quantity of rice,
flour, tea and masoor dhal (lentils) in this way. Some coconut
estates also sell coconuts at highly reduced prices to estate workers.
However, for all of this there is a very definite limit to the amount
of foodstuffs that can be obtained in this way if only because variations in the number of working days and in turnout rates affect income and in turn their repayment capacity.[28] Estate women are nevertheless very much in favour of such a system: it guarantees that
a larger proportion of the household's income is spent on household
necessities than might in other circumstances be the case.[29]

Other deductions from gross earnings prior to pay day come
from their contributions to the Employer's Provident Fund (10 per
cent of gross wages), union subscriptions, payments to the dhoby
(washerman) and the barber, and contributions for the upkeep of the
local temple. These are deducted automatically by the estate and
are fixed costs on the monthly salary of all registered workers.[30]
Also deducted are payments on outstanding debts to the estate by
the worker or his or her family.

At the end of this the worker receives a "net" wage which is very often considerably lower than the gross income outlined in the previous section. When the man collects this money one of the first outlays that he makes is likely to be the repayment of debts to a moneylender. These creditors are normally waiting nearby the pay office to receive what is owed to them and what they take can comprise a sizeable share of the net wage that the worker actually obtains. This is a topic that will be taken up again with rather more care in the following section.

Suffice it to say that the sum which still remains after these procedures is in the hands of the men, and that it is by no means uncommon to find them setting off from the pay desk to the tavern or to purchase bottles of drink from a petty trader. In this way drinking can account for at least 10 per cent of the net income that they collect, and it is clear from the interview evidence collected that there are very few men on the tea, rubber and coconut estates who do not drink and who do not adhere to this general pattern. Some women of the lower castes drink with the men, but this is gene- rally restricted to their homes (or to areas very near their homes) and it cannot be said to be of anything like the same proportions.

In this way the wages collected are whittled away and the money that is eventually available for other purchases is greatly reduced. Most of what remains is spent on household necessities, the main items being (more) rice, flour, dhal and tea, coriander, cumin, coco- nut oil, salt, onions, coconuts, vegetables, (occasionally) fish, sugar and other drinks. In addition kerosene oil has to be bought for cooking, beedis for smoking, betel nut for chewing, plus a certain amount for clothing and for entertainment. The latter is not so clearly a monthly expenditure as it tends to be associated with the celebration of festivals.

The proportion of this that is devoted to individual items is always to some extent at least a matter of taste. In general, how- ever, almost half the money spent on food is for flour and rice, 5-10 per cent on vegetables, lentils (dhal) and spices, the remainder being for the other items mentioned above.[31] Alcohol and smoking could account for up to 10 per cent of their monthly income, while festivals, clothing and other irregular items were very largely financed by way of loans.

To generalise a particular pattern of expenditure and consumption being valid for all of these estate workers would be to introduce an impression of homogeneity that does not exist, and that does away with the implications of economic, social and sexual differentiation

amongst the workers themselves.   However, bearing this in mind, it
is helpful to try and locate tendencies that are to be observed in
these expenditure patterns.   In order to do this a number of tables
have been constructed to gauge the nature of household expenditure
over time and income groups and to place it within the context of
the family.   In analysing them it should not be forgotten that who
receives what within the family is not revealed, and that women have
a disadvantaged position with regard to consumption patterns.

Table 4:   Detailed expenditure pattern for a
family of one male worker and two
female workers with three dependants
(a well off family) June 1980

	Rs.
40 kg rice at Rs. 4.20 a kg	168.00
60 kg flour at 5.25 a kg	313.00
1 kg chillies	31.00
5 kg Dhal at 12.25 a kg	61.25
Coriander 550 g	5.00
Cumin seed 200 g	6.00
Coconut oil 4 bottles	32.00
5 kg Salt at 1.00 per kg	5.00
1 kg onions	4.00
25 Coconuts at 1.50 each	37.50
Vegetables, fish, etc.	90.00
Kerosene oil 2 gallons	33.00
3 kg tea	3.00
Drinks, smoking, betel	110.00
5 kg Sugar at 13.23 a kg	66.15
Union subscription	6.00
Dhoby	7.50
Barber	2.00
	981.20

The expenditure listed in Table 4 does not include the amount
that is spent on entertainment, clothes and festivals.   As these
tend to occur far less regularly and are in most cases funded by
loans and debts, they have been omitted from these estimates of
monthly budgets.   The latter could nevertheless very easily be in
the range of Rs. 1,000 over the year.

As we have seen, family expenditure differs in relation to the
size of the family and the ratio of workers (who even when young
can be considered to consume more or less as much as an average
adult) to dependants.   It also varies between Tamils and Sinhalese,
and to indicate some of these characteristics certain averaged items
are tabulated below.

Table 5: Estimated average expenditure on food
          for families of different background
          and sizes (June 1980)

Item	Tamil family of six (four workers)	Tamil family of four (two workers)	Sinhalese family of seven
Rice (kg)	48	32	63
Flour (kg)	48	24	–
Dhal (kg)	1	1	3-4
Salt (kg)	4	2	5
Fish, Vegetables etc.	10 (Rs.)	2 (Rs.)	50 (Rs.)
Coconut oil (bottle)	4	2	3
Coconuts (No.)	30	20	50
Kerosene (bottle)	6	4	8
Tea (kg)	2	1	2
Sugar (kg)	very erratic as most people have drastically cut use because of the sharp increase in price.		
Spices (including onions)	10 (Rs.)	6 (Rs.)	10 (Rs.)
Drinks, betel, etc.	100 (Rs.)	50 (Rs.)	10 (Rs.)

Where significant qualitative changes are taking place (as in
the case of sugar) it is difficult to place any reliable figure
because people react to a sharp increase in price rather erratically.
differences between this and the previous table reveal, however,
that the modal income and expenditure pattern is towards the poorer
and consequently weaker dietary groups.

Even so, interpreting these estimates in terms of their
significance for standards of living is difficult without comparable
data to act as a benchmark or measure.   This is by no means easy

to acquire, as there have been few detailed analyses of consumption
and expenditure patterns amongst estate workers.[32] Nevertheless,
a first impression of the effects of price increases on the wages
of workers can be obtained by comparing price movements of their
main expenditure items with increases in wages, and this is quite
revealing.   For example, between 1960 and 1980 the minimum daily
wage amongst tea workers rose by approximately 278 per cent.   In
comparison the price of their main expenditure items rose as follows:

	per cent
Rice	137.5
Flour	715
Kerosene	1095
Coconuts	500
Coconut oil	887
Onions	900
Sugar	993
Cigarettes	700

Care has to be taken in drawing any conclusions from comparisons of this kind.   The relative weights of different items in the
household budget are very important, and in this respect the relative
decline in the price of rice is more significant than many other
increases.   No doubt this has helped to offset other price rises.
Nevertheless, it seems quite clear that, viewing their consumption
expenditure as a whole, it is extremely unlikely that there has
been any marked improvement and quite possible that it may actually
have seen a deterioration - and in some cases even a sharp deterioration over time.   The consumption of some items, such as kerosene,
is more or less constant and families may have been forced to concentrate on staples (and more particularly on rice rather than on
flour).

Looking at changes in the pattern of consumption a very similar
picture would seem to emerge.   Examining this in 1920 and 1980 in
which changes (if they had occurred) should have been very apparent,
the situation was interestingly enough found to have remained very
much the same.   Table 6 gives the average food costs per adult
worker as far back as 1923 (for Tamil tea workers).

Table 6 : The average cost of food for an
adult worker (Mr. Bateman's Budget, 1923)

	Cost Rs. Cts.	Tax Rs. Cts.
Rice, 40 lb	4.00	0.33
Salt, 1/2 measure	0.06	0.02 1/2
Kerosene oil, 1/4 bottle	0.06	0.00 1/2
Maldive fish, 1 1/2 lb	0.20	0.00 1/2
Dry fish, 1 1/2 lb	0.50	0.01
Dhal and green gram, 3 lb	0.38	0.01 1/2
Chillies, 3/4 lb	0.24	0.00 3/4
Other curry stuffs and onions	0.35	0.00 3/4
Sugar and jaggery, 1 1/4 lb	0.20	0.03
Soap	0.25	0.01 3/4
Cloth (average of the year)	0.75	0.04
Cloth (average per month)	0.30	-
Coconuts, 5	-	-
Coconut oil 1/4 bottle	0.23	-
Betel and vegetables	0.55	-
	8.07	0.52

Source: S.E.N. Nichols: Estate labour and legal guide (Colombo,
CAC 1927), p. 54.

It is clear from this that there has been an increase since
that time in the intake of wheatflour as well as in the quantity
of most other items. However, this dietary pattern has not changed
or improved very significantly: it reflects almost an identical
consumption pattern, and these changes are unlikely in practice to
have contributed very much to any improvement in dietary and nutritional standards.

The adequacy of this diet has in fact been seriously challenged
by several researchers. Severe anaemia, protein malnutrition and
undernutrition have been found to be both widespread and generalised
amongst estate workers and their families.[33] Furthermore, it has
been found that even today "chronic undernutrition occurred at a
markedly higher prevalence in estate children than in village
children".[34] The milk and triposha programme recently introduced by
UNICEF does seem to be improving the nutritional status of young
children, but it is clear that the basic family diet is far from
adequate.

Secondly, it became clear in the course of this research that food consumption per family member is inversely related to family size.   It is difficult to provide an adequate explanation of this phenomenon.   One factor could simply be the cost of feeding large families with a limited income.   However, it could also be that what is happening is roughly as follows.   As we have noted, the incomes of estate families tend to reach a cut-off point at about Rs. 1,200-1,300 at the time when the children begin to be full-time workers.   With a limit on income (albeit self-imposed), there is also a corresponding limit on the food they can purchase, and this occurs just at the time when "adult" children start eating more. In such a situation a decline in the consumption levels of individual family members is almost inevitable.   Furthermore, it has been established that there is a cultural trait amongst estate families whereby the woman gives the choicest food to the husband and then to the children.   In other words, if there is a decline in nutritional standards as a result of this trend to "cut off" the income it is the woman who is likely to suffer most.

Thirdly, it was found that comparing relatively rich and relatively poor estate families (and as we have seen there was a considerable difference from one to the other), there was also quite a difference in diet.   Where there was a need to cut down expenditure because the family was poor, the first sacrifice was in terms of wheatflour rather than rice (both of which are major items of diet). Conversely, as a family grew more wealthy they would purchase relatively more flour, and this provided them with a higher protein intake.   The diet of the poorer families was therefore worse.

Finally, in the case of non-resident workers the diet is somewhat better.   Firstly, the women collect the money, and that proportion which might otherwise be spent on liquor is spent on food. Secondly, their diet includes a larger proportion of vegetables, lentils and fish.   One way in which they overcome the difference between village and estate income is by cutting down on entertainment, clothing and smoking.   This seems to be broadly in keeping with the findings of the Nutrition Survey of 1976 to the effect that village children were better off in terms of nutrition than estate children.

Indebtedness

An important index of poverty amongst estate workers is their level of indebtedness.   There are several reasons that lead to this situation, but once they are in it the mechanisms of credit and debt are often manipulated in such a way that they cannot get out.   This is one reason for the prevalence and perpetuation of indebtedness, and because of this it seems to warrant particular attention.

Initially, people get into debt because credit is offered and because they have insufficient income at the time to meet their needs. This may be connected with the increasing rise in the price of essential commodities, with expenditures associated with customs and ceremonies or the ingenuity of the trader or moneylender who plays on the aspirations or sentiments of the labour force.   It is therefore important in assessing income and expenditure patterns to examine the nature of this indebtedness, the different responses on the part of those who get into debt and the way that this influences how people spend their money.

First, however, it is important to make clear just how prevalent indebtedness really is.   For example, over 98 per cent of the workers interviewed were in some form of debt.   Village studies on problems of poverty and indebtedness have also observed a high incidence of debt amongst the poorer groups in the Sinhalese villages, and since the non-resident labour comes from this category it seems reasonable to assume a high rate of indebtedness amongst them too.[35] In general the level of indebtedness amongst estate workers is very high.

The main sources of credit open to the estate worker are the estate management and the nearby boutique or kadai owner.   Workers obtain money or credit from the moneylender or trader at high rates of interests,[36] and by various subtle means they are kept at that level of debt.   For example, debtors are compelled to buy from the shop of the trader they have credit with, and the goods are sold to him at higher prices than those prevailing in co-operative stores. In some cases the boutique owner keeps the workers' "credit book"; purchases are not itemised and the fact that lump sums are not recorded and that there is ample scope for the books to be doctored when the debtor is away leaves the latter wide open to any abuse. Judging from the evidence collected in interviews these mechanisms served to keep an average debt in the range of Rs. 400-500, although individual cases varied as much as from Rs. 50 to Rs. 2,000.

If only because it is the man who does the shopping, this form
of credit is only available to men.   When the credit is substantial
the trader or moneylender is waiting near the paydesk to obtain his
dues.   In many cases, the worker hands over his pay to the creditor
to take what is owing; it is very difficult for him to evade this
collection procedure, and his level of literacy is often so low that
he is readily cheated.   However, one response that is open to such
a family is to increase the amount of foodstuff taken "on advance"
from the estates.   In this way the estate also becomes a creditor
albeit within strictly defined limits.   Indeed, it is interesting
to note that the poorer families with high rates of indebtedness
are those who take the most from the estates in terms of advances
thus avoiding some of the worst cheating of moneylenders.   The
worker who is not in debt (and therefore relatively well-to-do and
perhaps a moneylender himself) finds himself in a very different
position; he has more choice in deciding where to buy his foodstuffs
and gets more value for money.[37]

In the case of the non-resident women who did not have access
to traders' credit, a typical solution was to form a "seethu" fund.
This was a system whereby some 15 families would each contribute
Rs. 25 a month, and the total amount would be given to them in turn
or in cases of emergency to the one in need.

Over-all, the prevailing system of indebtedness had several
implications for women.   Firstly, it was yet another example of
the way in which her income was eaten away by other people.   Secondly,
when it came to pawning or selling to obtain further money or to
pay off debts, it was her jewellery that had to be sacrificed to
redeem the debts that had slowly accrued.   Finally, when debt repay-
ments cut into incomes and food consumption was reduced, it was
generally the woman who suffered most.

Although women may be ignorant of the details of debt repayment
they are well aware of - and indeed resent - the fact that they have
to pay for it in terms of their jewellery and other items of dowry.
This is viewed with a sense of loss and inevitability, accepting
the right of the husband to do as he wishes, as well as the need
for a form of alternative income in order to be able to obtain the
household necessities.

Quantification of the nature and extent of this indebtedness
and of its impact on women is very difficult to establish with any

really great degree of accuracy.   Nevertheless it is important,
its effects are hidden and tend to go by unknown.   The nature of
the different complex array of tendencies is such that it is in
need of much further conceptualisation and analysis.

Conclusions

A general conclusion which pervades any study of the income and
expenditure patterns of estate labour is that they are intrinsically
and strongly prejudicial to the interests of women.   The woman
sees few direct benefits for all her labours, and reaps a good many
ills.   If her priorities are different from those of her menfolk,
she has little opportunity to bring about change because she is
hemmed in by a cultural climate and traditional value system which
places her on a very secondary level.

Whether on the estate or in the home, she is confronted by a
structure of wage rates and by a division of labour that discrimi-
nates against her, by the man's claim to manage the household's
financial affairs and by a system of indebtedness for which she is
never herself directly responsible.   And yet, in almost all cases,
she is the one who suffers most.   Her wages are lower; she con-
tinues working long hours, even when the children are full-time
workers; she is the one who suffers from lower nutritional levels;
she suffers the loss of jewellery and dowry to pay off debts that
her husband has accumulated, and she suffers the violence when the
husband objects to her protests about what she endures.   It is in
this context that "household expenditure" and debt have to be seen.

Notes

[1] The latter may in practice entail payment in either cash or
kind.

[2] See K.P. Mukerjee: "The Ceylon Wages Board", in The Ceylon
Economist (Colombo), Vol. i. No. 2, 1950, pp. 115-123.   In the
case of State-owned plantations the Government performs a dual role.

[3] H.C. Abell: "Labour availability" (Position Paper No. 4 of
The Tea Master Plan Study, CIDA/Government of Sri Lanka, Colombo),
Oct. 1978, p. 17.

[4] Economic Review, Mar. 1980, p. 13.

[5] H. Abell, op. cit., p. 20.

[6] This is the number of days'work multiplied by the minimum wage using the data given on previous pages.

[7] The laboureres were still supposed to receive payment for 108 days, though in one estate that was visited this was not the case. The Chairman of the JEDB was quoted as saying in the Sunday Observer (Mar. 2 1980) that "We normally give six days work to our people but this has been reduced to four in some places. I know of private estates where they are giving only two days'work".

[8] For example, comparing hours worked and monthly earnings for the rubber industry between March 1975 and September 1976 reveals an increase in the rate per hour over this period that is considerably in excess of the increase in the minimum wage.

[9] For example, the evidence of Laboukellie estate:

Indices of days worked and earnings: (1979)

Sex	No.	Days worked	Earnings	Av. per day
Male	100	16.322	207.539	12.72
Female	100	16.591	133.574	8.12
Average	100	16.478	164.729	10.00

Source: Holiday Pay Book, 1979: Condagala Division, Laboukellie, Nuwara Eliya. Sample size 330 (the whole division).

[10] This can be illustrated by means of the following example which considers two cases where the norms are 8 kg and 15 kg respectively (this being the normal range of plucking norms).

Kilograms collected	Norm	No. of overkilos	Basic wage rate	Overkilo payment at Rs. 0.17 per kilogram	Actual rate per kilogram
4	8	--	7.23	0	1.80
8	8	--	7.23	0	0.90
12	8	4	7.23	0.68	0.65
15	8	7	7.23	1.19	0.56
21	8	13	7.23	2.21	0.45
9	15	--	7.23	0	0.80
12	15	--	7.23	0	0.60
15	15	--	7.23	0	0.48
18	15	3	7.23	0.51	0.43
19	15	4	7.23	0.68	0.34

[11] Refer to the examples given under footnote 1, p. 109.

[12] Rubber tappers are paid a varying rate per overkilo, namely Rs. 0.44 if their turnout is 100 per cent, Rs. 0.33 if it is 90-99 per cent, and Rs. 0.22 if it is 89 per cent or less. Sick days do not count in the calculation of this figure.

[13] This can be calculated as in the case of tea. With a norm of 4 kg a minimum wage of Rs. 15.59 and an overkilo rate of Rs. 0.44, the rate per kilogram for women collecting 3 kg and 7 kg respectively is Rs. 5.19 and Rs. 2.42. With a norm of 6 kg two women bringing in 5 kg and 9 kg are being paid an average of Rs. 3.12 and Rs. 1.88 per kilogram respectively. The rate of decline is faster in the former case.

[14] For a description of some of the problems facing workers in the coconut industry see Logos, Vol. 18, No. 1, 1979.

[15] "Non-estate" income refers to earnings other than those accruing from the normal activities of estate production that are paid by the management.

[16] In 36 estates in the Nuwara Eliya-Maskeliya electorate there were 263 hectares of line gardens. The total population of these estates was 56,865.

[17] On some estates families devoted nearly all their time to vegetable production and the management was struggling to evict them from the workers' lines as they were not doing estate work.

[18] On coconut estates superintendents often encourage cattle to graze in order to cut down on weeding costs. In the case of guarantees the worker is more or less bound to the estate until he has paid off the loan or until another has taken it on; repayment is made and controlled via the checkroll wage.

[19] Although this is done in only a few cases, they seem to have greater success.

[20] The level of unemployment in the villages is such that the scope for work of this kind is normally very limited indeed.

[21] This is based on a sample of workers from Spring Valley Estate, second division, in June 1980. In this range households varied from two to five working members.

[22] ibid.

[23] The lactation period for cattle is generally from four to six months, and vegetable production is by nature seasonal.

[24] This has been checked against estate income data for 330 workers (a complete division) on Labookellie Estate, Nuwara Eliya. This was based on incomes for an entire year (1979). Similar comparisons were made with smaller samples on several rubber estates. The earning potential in terms of overkilos, etc., is much less in the latter case, but this is compensated by the much higher minimum wage.

[25] In some cases this was so until they conceived and had children (and preferably a son); this would help to bridge the gap between her and her family, and she would again be accepted.

[26] One regional manager of the JEDB had worked on one estate comprised almost entirely of lower castes (pallans and paraiyans) and on one with a sizeable proportion of higher castes (vellalans). He maintained that there was a marked difference in the way that the women behaved with regard to financial matters. In the former the women collected their salaries and insisted on keeping them, while in the latter the men were in complete charge.

27 Workers are generally paid on the 10th of the month and food issues are made on the 25th.

28 On Spring Valley Estate, Badulla, the allowances in July 1980 were as follows: rice, 2 kg per person; flour, 2 kg per person per week (for both rice and flour, if the children are below 14 years of age the estates contributes Rs. 0.37 per kilogram); tea, 0.5 kg (at Rs. 0.40 per kilogram); and Masoor dhal, 1-2 kg per family.

29 In one instance where the union pressed for cash in lieu of kind the women did not agree because they would no longer have this assurance that the money would be spent on food.

30 Not all of these were compulsory; it depended on whether that particular service was wanted by the worker concerned. Apart from the EPF the other items deducted in July 1980 amounted to an average of approximately Rs. 8.50 per worker: union subscription Rs. 2, dhoby Rs. 2.50, barber Rs. 2.50, (not for women), temple up-keep Rs. 2 (not for the non-Hindus).

31 As the price of dhal was subsidised in the estate co-operatives or in estate sales, it was not uncommon to find cases of workers buying it and then turning it over to local shopkeepers for cash or for the repayment of loans.

32 The consumer price indices estimated on a macrolevel do not adequately reflect the consumption pattern of estate workers. For this reason we have been forced to resort to other means of comparison.

33 Economic Review, Mar. 1980, p. 16.

34 Sri Lanka Nutrition Survey, Colombo, 1976.

35 Survey of rural indebtedness (Central Bank, 1969); and W.M. Talakaratna: "Rural indebtedness in Ceylon", in Ceylon Economist (Colombo), Vol. IV, No. 2, 1958.

36 A figure of 5 per cent per month was frequently quoted during the interviews.

37 One such worker would buy rice in bulk, 100 kg at a time, from the town and was in this way able to obtain a better quality grain at a much lower price.

Chapter 6

WELFARE FACILITIES AND THE "WANTS" OF WOMEN

Over the years it has been increasingly recognised that women, as members of the estate labour force, should be entitled to certain benefits and welfare facilities designed to ameliorate the worst aspects of their situation and to eliminate many of the difficulties with which they are confronted. Most of these efforts have been more serious and more systematic in the post-nationalisation period, though the majority can in fact be traced back in one form or another to company days. There is no doubt that these facilities have made a difference in the lives of the women or that in many ways conditions have improved but even so the analysis of welfare facilities must be treated with care.

One important dimension of this over-all problem is the fact that the question of estate "welfare" has tended to be viewed in a rather conventional light and one which has not always succeeded in coming to terms with the peculiarities of the estate woman's situation. It tends to reflect a concern with "needs" as perceived by the management (and by conventional thinking on welfare services) rather than with the real "wants" of the woman herself. The latter of course are always difficult to estimate and the distinction between these two elements is not in practice quite as clear cut as this implies; many areas perceived as "needs" meet very real "wants", and on many issues the management is well informed of what women feel. Nevertheless, the fact that a potential distinction can exist has to be borne continually in mind in considering and assessing welfare facilities.

In this respect it is also necessary to look at the areas which are not considered to be in need of welfare services. Facilities are provided for crèches (to ease the problems of child care for working women), medical care (to help workers who are sick), housing (to provide them with accommodation on the estate, however bad), education (to make them literate), and family planning. Most of these themes have to do (at least in the longer term) with the efficient running of an estate and with the reproduction activities it needs in the broadest sense. What is not touched upon is the immediate condition of the woman in the household or in the community; there is less concern with the condition of the home itself or with widespread problems of physical and sexual violence which keep women

in a very submissive position.   The concern is in short with the
woman as a worker and not with the woman as a person with her personal
problems and her personal needs.   To some extent such concern
might be considered a luxury.   Many of these "personal" problems
have a long history and they are reinforced by deep-rooted cultural
values that are not easily changed.   But they are also elements that
facilitate differential wage rates and economic inequalities between
men and women issues which have been (and still are) important for
the plantation economy.   To be aware of this fact is to some extent
at least to reassess the question of welfare facilities in a rather
different light.

Be that as it may, it remains important to note (and to some
extent at least to evaluate) the very serious efforts that have in
practice been made to better the lot of the average plantation worker.
The various welfare facilities that have been provided will therefore
be examined here one by one.

Crèche facilities

Even when young children are well they still pose certain
problems for the working mother.   More specifically they impede
her work on the estate because it is she who is responsible for their
welfare   In this respect, access to crèche facilities has always
been considered an important issue.   In the past and in many areas
today, crèches are held in old line rooms or sheds kept apart for this
purpose, with an old woman (usually a retired or disabled tea plucker)
hired to look after the children while their mothers work.   Even
today there are still very few "upgraded" crèches on the estates,
though the need for them is widely recognised in management circles
and considerable assistance has been given by UNICEF to set them up.[1]
The "upgraded" crèches that have been established have far better
facilities in terms of buildings, sanitation and water facilities,
food and cooking facilities, toys and educational materials.   The
crèche attendants are also trained in the majority of cases.[2]

When the women are asked why they do or do not use the crèches,
a very clear pattern of responses seems to emerge   The resident
population uses the crèche if there is one - and it is not always
the case that one exists - because it is convenient, because of the
facilities that are available (particularly free milk), and in some
cases, because they appreciate the work of the crèche attendant.

This does not necessarily mean, however, that it is the "upgraded" crèches which always have the highest attendance. The non-resident workers do not in general avail themselves of crèche facilities.

Non-attendance is normally due to several factors. First is the question of distance and whether the woman can get the child to the crèche and report for work in time without too much difficulty. In many cases this is simply not possible given the workload of the woman and the limited time that she has available for it and this is especially true in the case of the Sinhalese women who come from the village. Secondly, the condition of the crèche is often a determining factor, particularly when it rains. Most of the old crèches are badly maintained; they have leaking roofs, no running water, inadequate space and very rarely any other facilities. Even today the majority of the crèches are still in this condition.

A third factor is the training or attitude of the crèche attendant. In the old crèches, attendants do not always know how to look after so many children or are unable to do so because of their ill-health, old age or of some infirmity. In "upgraded" crèches the situation is rather different; women are often appointed from outside the estate community under political influence and they often cannot speak the language of the children they are looking after. It is hardly surprising therefore that in certain instances misunderstandings and dissatisfaction on the part of the resident population should be the result. Finally, lack of interest in their work on the part of crèche attendants who see their work as no more than a source of employment, means that they put little effort into their work, into discussion with parents or into encouraging parents to use the facilities which are available.[3]

Not all the attendants treat their work in such a manner. Many put in a very serious effort and they in contrast have tended to be very successful in stimulating enthusiasm amongst the workers.[4] In the end, however, the key factors tended to be whether a crèche existed and whether a particular woman had other alternatives. Much depended on the interest of the superintendents; in all the cases where the attendants were able to arrange something out of the ordinary, this tended to be received with the parents' strong approval and support. In the matter of alternatives, much depends on whether the woman has older children or relatives to do this work. In the case of non-residents where the distance from the estate is such that they have to leave very early to reach their work in time, women have little choice but to rely on such solutions.

In short, given the division of labour and established logic
of estate employment, it is essential for a working woman to find a
solution to the problem of minding young children   For many women
the only options that are realistically open to them are to keep an
older child (almost invariably a girl) away from school, thus fore-
going her own chance of a good education or of putting her young
child into a crèche where he or she receives inadequate care with
meagre facilities.   Both of these work to the advantage
of the estate and to the disadvantage of children.   Whether it is
an old or an "upgraded" crèche, the mother has no say in the kinds
of facilities that are offered.   She either has to accept what is
given or to deprive one of her daughters of some education - unless
she can take advantage of some other relative.

Medical facilities

The knowledge and attitude of the estate woman to medical
facilities and her access to them vary quite considerably from area
to area.   In Sri Lanka good estate hospitals are comparatively rare
and they tend to be concentrated in certain pockets in the up-country
tea areas.   When there are good estate hospitals and doctors (or
EMAs) there, resident women prefer to attend them because they are
more accessible both in geographical and in social terms.[5]   Where
estate hospitals have been upgraded the women also appreciate the
fact and turn to them more;   non-resident women tend not to go to
hospital elsewhere.

It is only when there is no estate hospital, or when the case
is serious enough to warrant more specialised attention that resident
workers are passed on to the government hospitals.   Often these are
located at a considerable distance from the estate and - with exception of the more serious cases - workers have to walk or to catch a
bus to seek attention.   In serious cases the estate provides transport for the patient though this is a service that - rightly or
wrongly - is a subject of continual complaints.[6]   In the low-country
areas government hospitals are far more accessible and more frequently
used.   Estate hospitals are consequently fewer in number.   If they
do exist, then they are also available to Sinhalese villagers (a
policy that is being promoted by the present Government to integrate
the estates more into Sinhalese society).   However, it was clear
from interviews with Sinhalese women that, whatever the principle,
most of them were not aware that these hospitals could be used by
their kith and kin and they rarely used them.

In addition to the hospitals, which are not so frequent, most estates have a dispensary that is supposed to be sufficiently equipped to deal with minor ailments and minor infections.[7] These are manned by the EMAs officials with a para-medical training. Recently, the (JEDB) estate management has embarked on a policy of rationalisation where one EMA caters for several estates rather than for one as in the past. The effect of this on the service that is being provided is difficult to assess, but it is clear that many women feel that quality has since declined. The information available to workers was not always effective; in some cases they did not even know if (or when) they had access to an EMA.

In general, the complaints most frequently voiced were three in number:

    (i)   that transport to hospital was simply not available, or simply not adequate when it came to cases of serious need;

    (ii) that there were insufficient medicines available; and

    (iii) that the "cures" that they were given were no more than temporary cures, often recurring after a short period of time.

The question of transport is a difficult one to assess as it is probably true that the lorry is called at the very last moment and then needed at once. But there is no doubt that transport at that moment of need is a serious problem and that it often leads to unnecessary discomfort and worry for a great many patients. Similarly, in the case of medicines, it is by no means uncommon to hear from women that they attended an estate hospital but then had to travel to town to buy the necessary drugs. Finally, in the case of recurrent illness, it is not clear whether this recurrence was a reflection on the nature of the work, the adequacy of the treatment, the extent to which the patient followed the prescribed treatment, the unhygienic conditions under which they lived, the chronic poor quality of water and water shortage, their general state of mal- or undernutrition or a combination of these and other factors.[8] Yet the point remains, and remains a significant one, that the women experienced recurrent illnesses. The treatment they received was simply enough to get them back in the fields. Asked if there had been an improvement in medical facilities, the women tended to reply that there had been very little. Some of the older women even went so far as to say that the situation had deteriorated, although how far this is true is very hard to assess.

Having said this, one facility which is particularly of concern
to women is the maternity service and for this reason it warrants
some separate attention.   Firstly, separate maternity wards are
provided in hospitals; women are asked to come to the hospital a
few days before the birth and to remain there under care for a few
days after.   If it is necessary the medical officer will even keep
them there for some time longer.   Secondly, nurses and experienced
midwives are present either from their own people or from the village.
Conditions are good (certainly in comparison with home conditions),
the treatment is adequate (providing the birth takes place without
complications) and the woman is given a valuable break from the
drudgery of her ordinary life during this period.   Thirdly, food,
drugs and other services are (as in the case of estate hospitals in
general) paid by the estate.   Fourthly, the woman receives a maternity benefit equivalent to 42 days' pay to help her recover,[9] though
how far the money is used in this way is open to doubt.   The
Maternity Benefit Ordinance No. 32 of 1939 allowed for the nomination
of persons to collect this benefit and it is common for husbands to
go and collect it.   As in the case of wages, this often implies that
the women have no control over how the money is spent.   It is not
uncommon to find that she receives very little benefit and that much
is spent on clearing debts and on drinking.   Finally, with the
important exception of the transport problem, none of the women had
complaints about these services.   Infantile mortality rates and
death rates of mothers have shown a marked decline in the entire
estate sector; women prefer to have their children in hospitals
if they can.

The main sickness of which women workers complained seemed
related to the environmental conditions under which they were forced
to live and work.   There are several illnesses that are common to
estate labour in general although variations occur depending on a
series of factors such as the age of the worker, the climate in the
area of the estate, the nature of the work that she undertakes and
whether or not she is resident on the estate.

The most frequent illnesses are bowel disorders, stomach pains
and stomach trouble (which tend to be associated with bad drinking
water and inadequate sanitary conditions), boils, fever and headaches.   In the up-country tea areas women complain, in the colder
and wetter parts, of coughs, chest pains, shivering and difficulties
in breathing.   In the hotter parts of the year (for example, in

Badulla), they complain of pain and swelling of the neck, dizziness
and unconsciousness due to their exposure to the sun day after day.
Vaginal discharge is prevalent everywhere and backpains are common
amongst rubber tappers.[10] Non-residents mention in addition leg,
hand and body pains which are often due to the fact that they are
new to the estates and not used to the work. In general young
women tend to be more healthy than their elders; working under
rigorous climatic conditions might well have an invigorating effect
on the body, but it is also a formula for growing old quickly and
gradually weakening.

When they are ill, workers go to the dispensary or, in cases
of emergency, to the nearest hospital However, the majority just
take disprin and carry on to avoid losing work. When the medicines
which they need are not available nearby some men go and buy them
for their wives. Since most of the Sinhalese who were interviewed
did not have menfolk they had to rely on their children to help them
out, especially their daughters. However, they are more likely to
have relatives near at hand and the latter will help when both mother
and child are sick. This was not the case with the Tamils: except
for the mother and father, these women were unable to rely on the
help of other relatives in dealing with problems arising from day-
to-day illnesses. This reliance on immediate female family members
to care for the sick is very much part of the traditional pattern
and it appears to have undergone very little change over the years.

How often illness keeps the estate woman from work depends
(a) on her general state of health, (b) on whether she has children
at home and whether she has older children to look after the young
when they are sick, and (c) on the age of the particular woman concerned These points are interrelated and form a vicious circle.
The health of a woman determines her ability to work and only in
serious cases is she likely to stay away. When she is young, her
health will in general tend to be better, but at this age she is
likely to have young children who are frequently sick. When they
are very young, she stays away from work in order to look after
them; when the children grow up, the elder daughter stays away from
school to look after the younger children, and when all the children
have grown up they look after themselves. However, by this time
the woman herself will have reached an age when work has taken its
toll; she is as a result more prone to illness and she may be less
able to work because of her own health problems.[11]

Housing conditions

The housing conditions of estate labour have long been
identified as not only a serious but also a sensitive issue.[12]
The enormity of the problem has to be appreciated, involving a need
to improve something in the range of a quarter of a million housing
units.[13]   The task of improving it is therefore an enormous one
and it is only recently that policies have been introduced aiming to
ameliorate the situation.[14]

Legally, a single line room may not house more than two adults
and three children under 12 years.   A double room cottage should
not accommodate more than 4 adults and 4 children under 12 years of
age.[15]   This is a "minimum" solution to the housing problem since
most of the rooms available are extremely small.   According to the
Department of Labour, 90 per cent of the estate labour force live
in line rooms.[16]   The earlier Socio-economic survey of Ceylon,
1969/70 gave a similar figure of 89 per cent of the people living
on the estates housed in "labour lines", barrack-like structures
with 10-12 small units under one roof.[17]   Many of these lines have
remained little changed for the last 100 years[18] with rooms
12 x 10 feet, one door and at best one window and a small kitchen
area, the accommodation is abysmal and generally overcrowded.   One
observer maintained that in an estate near Nuwara Eliya, 30 families
were living huddled and congested in 14 rooms.[19]   My observations
suggest that this is exceptional and that while there are very many
cases of more than one family occupying one room, the majority tend
to be one family dwellings.[20]   Even so, this is by no means grounds
for congratulation and despite the departures due to repatriation,
the number of occupants per room appears to be increasing.[21]

Many of the women who were interviewed had been living in the
same line room for 30 or 35 years.   Their whole lives had been
carried out under these conditions.   It is hardly surprising therefore that housing was for them a vehement source of complaint.   The
main areas of discontent were the lack of space and the perennial
problem of water supply.[22]   Other problems were poor sanitation
conditions, smell from latrines, holes in the walls, leaking roofs,
broken doors and windows which occurred largely because of the lack
of maintenance.[23]   Not all of these problems occurred simultaneously
on all the estates and although some have appeared to the management
to be minor issues, they had a considerable bearing on the day-to-
day life of the estate woman.

It seems that there have been some improvements in the last generation. Some of the older women said that they now have cooking facilities which were not there in the past; some new cottage houses have been constructed and there seems to have been an increase in the number of kitchen gardens. However, seen over a period of years - let alone over a generation - these improvements were really quite minimal, and they have scarcely affected the life of the average worker. Kitchen facilities are scarcely very much better, and cottage houses tend to be taken over by junior staff.[24]

In interpreting the significance of accommodation and sanitary facilities it has to be borne in mind that the person principally affected is generally the woman. She is the one responsible for the household work; the kind of accommodation has a direct effect on her tasks since it provides the environment in which she spends so much more of her time. If there is no water nearby, she must fetch it; if the drains are blocked, she is the one who is working by smelly drains; in short, if the accommodation is in practice inadequate, it simply places another burden upon her life. The men can find for themselves a more pleasant location.

In the case of the non-resident workers who have not been allocated homes on the estate, the housing situation is somewhat different. Many of them have qualified for government assistance schemes, and those who have not encroached on land (and there are some who have) do not experience the same housing difficulties as the resident labour. On the other hand, the structure of their dwellings is not very sound and they often face difficulties on that score.

Education

Analysis of the educational pattern of the estate workers has to bear in mind the way in which the traditional family structure responds to economic need and the way in which non-formal "education" imbibes in them an acceptance of their traditional role. In this the most important factors are the division of labour within the household (which, as we have seen, associates women with household work), the ideology which considers her inferior and the way these two factors shape responses in times of economic distress. When it comes to schooling they combine to work against the women on the estates.

Firstly, in the case of the resident labour force, it has been economically important for all family members to work on the estate. Furthermore, they have been strongly encouraged to do so both by their own menfolk and by the estate management. In addition to this, the woman has to look after the household work until, if she has a daughter who is old enough (and she is "old enough" from as young as 7 or 8 years), the daughter begins to take on much of the work "because she is a girl". She has to clean the house, prepare the food and look after the younger children because her mother is tired and because this is the tradition, thus relieving the older woman of some of her chores. This the girl does at the expense of her education. It is considered a "natural" role for a daughter to perform.

Secondly, many families interviewed said that for them the costs involved in sending a child to school were a heavy burden. This they viewed in terms of the items that had to be bought and of wages forgone. The response to this economic pressure was such that most families tended to give preference to the schooling of boys. The future of the girl was treated as a matter of far less importance as she would marry and because her future was seen as being limited to tea plucking or rubber tapping. This was a view that was gradually engrained in her way of thinking and it was simply accepted that it was only the man who had a chance of bettering his situation. This was generally true of the resident population.

Thirdly, in the case of non-resident labour the educational achievements of women appear to be linked to the process of pauperisation taking place in the villages.[25] A common response on the part of the poor was, as we have seen, that their women had to seek employment outside the home. Thus while literacy exists to some extent amongst the older women, it is practically non-existent among very young women who have only recently begun to work on the estates. In short, as the economic situation in the villages deteriorated, women were forced out to work at an earlier age and this in practice had serious implications in terms of their educational opportunities and educational achievements.

The upshot of all of this is that educational patterns tend to reconfirm a woman's inferior position. Women are far less educated than men; while over 98 per cent of the women who were interviewed could neither read nor write, all the men could read and a great many had minimum writing skills as well. This pattern

is confirmed by a comparison of their levels and years of study.
Men tend on the average to have studied longer and to have attained
higher levels of education.   This has tended to place the woman at
a further disadvantage, since on so many issues she has to depend
on the skills of the man.   The estate women have the lowest levels
of literacy in the country,[26] many of them cannot even read the
weighing scales that record the tea that they have picked or the
rubber that they have tapped.

Until recently the schools were run by the estate management
which was known on many occasions to take the view that their
purpose was to keep the children occupied rather than to provide
them with meaningful education.[27]   Some superintendents saw education as a potential threat to their labour force in that educated
people, particularly women, would be more reluctant to work on the
estates under present conditions.   With the Land Reform of 1975,
the estate schools were taken over by the Educational Department in
a step-by-step process.   As yet, this process is not complete,
and there is very little positive change to be observed.   In some
districts, reorganisation has meant the closure of schools often
with little consideration for the distances that children have to
travel.   The resources channelled into the upgrading of estate
schools have not been sufficient to have any impact on standards in
estate schools as a whole.[28]   Attendance rates have deteriorated[29]
and superintendents who might earlier have acted on this situation
now find that it lies outside their jurisdiction and pay no heed.
This may well be a transitional period, the conditions improving
once the take-over and reorganisation is completed.   However, it
is by no means sure at all that this will be the case.

On the whole, estate schools have classes up to Grade V,
although many children fail to progress that far.   Drop-out rates
are high, even as early as second or third grade, especially for
girls.   What is more, in the view of at least one commentator the
education they receive is more suitable for the potential white-
collar worker than for someone who is working in agriculture, and
given the prevailing value system of these people, it is one more
relevant for boys than it is for girls.[30]

When asked what type of employment they would like their
children to acquire, women workers resident on the estates said
that they would like their sons to obtain better employment within
the estate and that education was important for this.   They

recognised the importance of education for girls, but at the same time, the system of work was such that in their eyes they needed their daughters' help within the house and saw little chance of them better-ing their position.

Non-residents hoped that their sons and daughters would eventually be able to reach a situation where they would not have to work on estates at all; their aspirations lay with government jobs, but they saw little opportunity given high unemployment rates and their disadvantaged position in local society.

Family planning

Estate workers have become increasingly aware of the possibility of family planning during the last decade and they have done so largely as a result of the Government's efforts. Nevertheless, the information they have is almost entirely limited to tubectomy and vasectomy. In short, the stress is placed on terminating rather than on controlling their fertility. The management would appear to espouse the view that this is the only effective method of birth control for estate workers.

No information is provided to unmarried women about family planning; no doubt information is available, but the policy stress is clearly on married women and in their social system it is diffi-cult for a single woman to be seen inquiring. As a result, unmarried women are very ignorant of birth control methods,[31] and consequently, it was not uncommon for unmarried women to have children for which they were almost invariably left with the responsi-bility.

The estate women want to have children. Children provide them with additional income, ease their workload in the house, and look after them when they are sick and when they are old. However, there comes a point when all the children require some care and the cost involved becomes a burden. Most women said that the cost of bring-ing up children is such that they can no longer afford to have large families.

On the other hand, neither the man nor the woman easily accept the idea of an operation. Both are, understandably enough, appre-hensive about it and they associate it with post-operational problems.[32] The men in particular seem to feel that a vasectomy

implies a certain loss of manliness and self-esteem.   However, it
is the woman who is faced with the day-to-day pressures of bringing
up children;   she bears not only the financial but the physical and
psychological pressures of making ends meet.   She has little time
in the course of her working day to get advice on the alternative
methods of birth control which are available.   The estate management pays up to Rs. 500 to a woman to undergo a tubectomy compared
to only Rs. 250 for a vasectomy in the case of a man.[33]   And
altogether this series of factors tends to push the woman into
having a tubectomy, whatever doubts and reservations she might have.

Discussions with the estate welfare officers that have recently
been appointed on a few estates tend to confirm this general pattern.
They emphasised the fact that the women had little chance to obtain
information on family planning during their working day and that they
were worried about the prospect of being unwell and losing their work
after the operation had been performed.   They also maintained that
with more time for discussion many of the fears and reservations of
the workers could be allayed, that if the woman were given lighter
tasks for a while after the operation, they would be more willing to
undergo it and that birth control practice in general could be
improved in this way.

However, the welfare officers and the estate management had
little to say about other methods or about shifting more responsibility for birth control on to the men.   The value system of the
estate communities tended to stress control of women's reproductive
functions;   men said that if the woman had a tubectomy, even if she
was unfaithful there would be no children and he would be spared
that disgrace;   but if he had a vasectomy and the woman had children
he would lose face.[34]   Moreover, for them the fertility of the man
was important in case they should ever want another wife.   In all
of this, arguments weighed heavily in favour of tubectomy and against
the woman.   It was the woman's fertility that had to be terminated
and to be controlled.

The themes discussed above cover the main areas in which
"welfare services" in the conventional use of the term have been
provided.   It is clear that over the years considerable changes
have taken place, and that many of them have worked as much to the
advantage of women workers as of the men.   Moreover, after so many
years of comparative neglect, the magnitude of many of the problems
in areas such as housing is of such proportions that they could

scarcely be overhauled in a short period of time. The costs would
in practice be far too high in both economic and political terms.

And yet, at the same time, it is quickly apparent from the
materials available and from visits to the estates that, of all
the areas that have experienced change, the personal life of the
woman has probably been the one that has changed the least. Not
only is her working day (particulary on tea estates) arduous and
extremely tiring, but she is also the one who bears the burden of
the household chores, she is the one most likely to take the brunt
of any decline in dietary standards and she is the one who works
while others "retire" when incomes increase. She is the one affected
most by bad housing and sanitary conditions and who bears the additional burdens when the children are sick. All of this raises
question marks which range far beyond the familiar matter of unequal
wages and which really concern the "welfare" of the estate woman.
Over and above all of this there is one particularly important
additional issue which stands out and which is in need of consideration and that is the whole question of physical violence.

Women and violence in estate society

One of the consequences of women being in such an inferior
position has been that they have more easily been the subject of
abuse. This abuse, in the form of threats and physical violence,
has had a long history in plantation agriculture and plantation
society, as we have already seen. To a large extent it has always
been seen a domestic matter, something private, and something which
with the exception of the most extreme cases was no business at all
of society at large. This attitude has been reinforced and made all
the more strong by the whole ideology of patriarchy and by the division of labour which it implied.

From the first introduction of female slaves to satisfy the
sexual frustrations of the estate men (be they of the management
or of the labour force), violence has been very much a part of their
lives. Their use for the needs of sexual gratification, "to keep
workers content", was as we have seen a part of the whole question
of labour control. Serious injury resulting from fights over women
are well noted in records relating to Sri Lankan plantations.[35]
Since it was invariably the most extreme of these cases that were

considered worthy of notice, it seems quite likely that the problems of violence and sexual abuse involving women were far more general than is often suspected and they were never a part of the "welfare" considerations.

On the contemporary plantations physical violence between men and women is still an extremely common phenomenon. Indeed, it is an almost universal feature of plantation life. To some extent the cramped conditions and unvaried pattern of an estate existence may have a bearing on this, but the fact remains that over 75 per cent of the women interviewed made the point that they had been beaten. Superintendents confirmed this point, and when it is borne in mind that this violence contains for the woman an element of disgrace and is a matter that is often too embarrassing to disclose to outsiders let alone discuss, it seems clear that it is a wide-spread and important issue.

Beatings seem to be a little less common (or less revealed) amongst higher caste groups, perhaps because the "provocation" is that much less, or the family has more of an image that it tries to keep up but it was still found to be a rather prevalent feature. The Sinhalese women were more likely to have had a love than an arranged marriage and, living off the estate, they could more easily hide the fact that such things occurred But occur they did. On the estates the fact that there were beatings was very well known (indeed it would often have been very hard to have hidden the fact), but it was widely accepted within the community as their way of life.

Beatings occurred the most when men had been drinking. The basic cause sparking off particular incidents was frequently a minor one (at least to the outsider) - the food she had prepared was not found to be tasty enough, she woke up late, she did not serve the man in the way that he wanted her to, or because she said she did not like him spending their money on liquor. The woman was likely to be beaten at any time when the man felt that respect for him and his authority was being brought into question or when he had no verbal retort to an argument and knew he was lost. Sexual violence was also not uncommon and fights based on jealousy and suspicion often led to injuries of a serious nature. Women were often forced to have sexual intercourse against their will and any show of defiance was met with violence.

This violence was and still is a very real part of the every-
day life of the estate women. It is known to occur widely (and
known to occur so even in management circles) and it is accepted
as bad; but nothing is done to change this course of events.
Violence within the family or elsewhere on the estate is seen as
something that is private as indeed it is in many other parts of the
world; but here it is without the broader means of protection by
society at large Violence is almost considered as being a right
of the man concerned, whether this man is the husband, the lover,
the kangany or the estate superintendent. Today, if only because
of the growing power of estate trade unions, abuse by the management
has more or less disappeared. But it is a prevalent feature of
the life of the female worker and one that has to be seen as yet
another element in a long series of controls that are placed upon
her on an emotional, psychological or social plane.

Notes

[1] See UNICEF: Services for children in the estate areas
(Colombo, n.d.) which outlines the programme of collaboration with
the Sri Lankan Government. This programme started in 1979.
"Upgraded" crèches that I have visited are solid buildings roughly
6 x 4 metres with a separate kitchen area, (usually) running water,
a smooth separate toilet. The materials at hand depend to a large
extent (as always) on the initiative of the crèche attendant, but
they are generally good. Milk is provided (mixed from powder) and
the water is carefully boiled before it is used. The cups, spoons,
and other utensils are provided by UNICEF and with the upsurge of
enthusiasm recently cooking facilities have been provided by many
estates. Simple toys have also been made available and if the
crèches are still in some cases rather stark, they are an enormous
improvement on those which they have replaced.

[2] Although many of these women are still untrained, it is
established policy gradually to train them. Suitable candidates,
to be recruited by the estate management, are to be (a) young women
between 21 and 40 years of age who (b) have at least passed Grace VII,
with preference given to those who have GCE "O" level. See UNICEF,
op. cit., p. 75.

[3] In the case of one estate in the up-country areas with 418
children under the age of 16 and an upgraded crèche, only one or two
children attended each day. Since it was located near to the lines,
this did not seem to be in any way a matter of distance.

[4] One estate attendant, for example, in a low-country rubber
estate organised an excursion for the children about which the parents
were extremely enthusiastic. In another (coconut) estate efforts
had been made to provide the children with clothing for use in the
crèche so that they were clean during the day. This again was
greeted with appreciation.

[5] The EMA is an "Estate Medical Assistant".

[6] The point here is that complaints about the inadequacy of transport, about the reluctance of the estate to provide transport and about the lorry or tractor arriving late were invariably countermanded by accusations that requests came at the last minute when cases were already severe and that transport was asked at times when it was not really essential.

[7] The normal budgetary allowance from the Government for drugs is Rs. 0.50 per worker per year, a figure which is unanimously agreed to be quite inadequate, and which has been unchanged for years. The additional costs for drugs are met from the estates' own budget.

[8] In short, it could well be that the estate management has tended to place too much emphasis upon medical infrastructure rather than on the quality of the service rendered. This, however, is no more than an impression on my part, though it has support from some members of the medical profession who have worked on estates. It could be added that qualified medical practitioners tend to look askance at the EMAs.

[9] This is calculated on the following basis. If there is no maternity ward the payment is = (wage rate) x 42 x 6/7 = Rs. 330.84 (in the case of tea). If a maternity ward is available payment is = Rs. 330.84 - 3/7(330.84) = Rs. 189.09. Up to 1972 if a woman had not worked for 150 days prior to the birth she would get only Rs. 8. Under the Act No. 13 of 1978 dated 5 December 1978 workers who have worked for even one day will qualify for full maternity benefit.

[10] Doctors generally associated vaginal discharge with bad hygiene associated with poor sanitary conditions and water supplies.

[11] Field work has revealed that in the case of Tamils, 30-50 per cent of working days which were lost were due to the illness of children and although the proportion was about the same for the Sinhalese they tended to work for fewer days on the estates. If anything the Tamils lost slightly more time because their children tended to be sick more often as well.

[12] Legislative Council Debates, 24 February 1927, pp. 357-381.

[13] Socio-economic survey of Ceylon (Colombo) 1969/70, Department of Census and Statistics.

[14] Construction of twin cottage and conversion of existing line rooms to semi-detached cottages, each category providing a floor space of 480 sq. ft., Labour Gazette, Colombo, Ministry of Labour: May Day supplement 1979, p. 189.

[15] Instructed under the Disease (Labourers) Ordinance of 1961, section 12, chapter 175.

[16] Labour Gazette, May Day Supplement, op. cit., p. 139.

[17] *Socio-economic survey of Ceylon*, 1969/70, op. cit.

[18] See the Medical Wants Ordinance of 1872, *Report by the Inspector of Estates of 1876*, in *Legislative Council Debates*, 24 February 1927, p. 357f.

[19] Edith Bond: *The State of Tea*, March 1974, p. 9.

[20] *The Socio-economic survey of Ceylon*, 1969-70, estimated an average occupancy of 5.1 persons per line room.

[21] This is because of the high level of natural increase, the slow rate of repatriation and the demolition or closure of the "back-to-back" lines on some estates.

[22] On average some 30-35 people would be using one tap; in many cases there was no water and women had to carry it, either because the piping was damaged or because it was stolen.

[23] These complaints were quite prevalent on the estates which were visited.

[24] It was argued by the estate management that workers were reluctant to move into cottage houses.

[25] On this see the *Report of the Kandyan Peasantry Commission*, Sessional Paper XVIII of 1951.

[26] *Socio-economic survey of Ceylon*, 1969/70. While the gap between urban and rural areas is not very great in terms of literacy, the estate sector stands out for its illiteracy levels.

[27] *Economic Review*, March 1980, p. 17. The lack of progress in education on the estates, whereby a worker's child had little chance of proceeding beyond the fifth grade, has also been observed in ILO: *Matching employment opportunities and expectations: A programme of action for Ceylon* (Geneva, 1971), p. 10, footnote 2.

[28.] *Economic Review*, op. cit., p. 17.

[29] The poor attendance refers not only to the pupils but also to teachers since they no longer have the superintendent at hand supervising activities.

[30] Bond, op. cit., p. 10.

[31] In many cases the ignorance of unmarried women was 100 per cent. This was particularly so in the case of the Sinhalese.

[32] Both men and women complained of feeling weak after the operation, though it is difficult to assess if this was more than psychological. Women also complained of headaches, abdominal and stomach pains, continual bleeding and general lethargy.

[33] The older women grumbled that they had only been paid in the past, showing the importance to them of financial incentives. They were given seven days' paid leave for tubectomy and three days for a vasectomy.   From 1 March 1979, the rates were as follows:

For female sterilisation:

(a)   for those consenting to sterilisation after the first, second and third child, Rs. 500 plus seven days' paid leave.

(b)   for those consenting to sterilisation after the fourth child, Rs. 300 plus seven days' paid leave.

For male sterilisation, Rs. 250 and three days' paid leave.

[34] These comments are based on interviews with male labourers on the estates.   Men were questioned with a view to establishing checks on the information obtained from the women.

[35] See W. Sabonadière: The coffee planter of Ceylon (Colombo, Messrs. Green and Co., 1866), p. 85;   and Administrative Reports, 1899, Report of the Government Agent for the Central Province, pp. C-15 and C-23.

Chapter 7

TRADE UNIONISATION

The options that are open to the estate workers to better
their position are not very numerous. Some have preferred to
leave Sri Lanka and to return to India in the context of the recent
policies of repatriation. Most of the upper castes left because
they were the ones who had acquired land or had built up savings or
other connections in India, and because it was easier for them to
some extent at least to begin to find their own way and to begin
again. Even so many of the lower castes had also returned.
Families went because the man had wanted to go; in the vast majority
of such cases the man made the decision, the man received the necessary papers and the stipulated settlements (Employment Provident
Funds, etc.), and the women left the estate in the same situation as
they had been on it - entirely dependent upon the goodwill of their
men.

For those who remained conditions were difficult. Whether
Tamils or Sinhalese, they were people who were very vulnerable and
who were in no position to press for a change in their situation
other than through the representations of formal workers' organisations, namely the trade unions. In this sense the trade unions
were (and still are) of quite crucial importance and those to which
the vast majority of estate workers belong are amongst the most
powerful trade unions in the country.[1] Their influence, attitudes
and achievements are therefore important in assessing possible avenues
of change for plantation people.

According to an International Labour Office report of 1976[2]
some 80 per cent of plantation workers belonged to trade unions, the
largest and most influential of which are the Ceylon Workers Congress,
the Lanka Jathika Estate Workers Union and the Lanka Estate Workers
Union. At least half the membership of these unions is comprised
of women and they are therefore a channel whereby (theoretically
at least) women have an opportunity to air their grievances and to
negotiate with the management to bring about change. Many of the
problems which these women encounter in the course of their estate
work and their lives on estates fall within the purview of these
trade unions whether this concerns questions of wages, working
conditions, water or housing. How forceful are the unions in taking
up their problems?

There can be no doubt that the unions have achieved a great
deal for estate labour in general.   Serious and consistent work has
been done on their behalf and there has been notable improvement in
incomes and the work situation.   This is an achievement that must
be emphasised.   However, they have been much less successful in
taking up issues specific to women or to their day-to-day lives.
Differential wages for the same task on the basis of sex are found
at all levels;   in some areas such as tea plucking and rubber tapping
(which involve most of the women) the injustice of this is widely
acknowledged throughout the estate management and yet it has only
recently been taken up as a relevant issue by some trade unions and
so far at least with little effect.   Nor, as we have seen, has much
been done to improve their housing.   And in areas where notable
changes (as with the crèches) have occurred, the initiative was not
to come from the union but from outside.   These are by no means
easy tasks to be tackled.   Many other basic rights have had to be
gained for workers in general and the fact that unions tend to give
low priority to the interests of women is not confined to Sri Lanka
nor indeed to the Third World.   Nevertheless, why this is so in
the Sri Lankan case warrants attention and it has to be understood
by examining how these women come to join the trade unions, the
extent of their participation and the nature of the traditional
union organisation.

Firstly, the question of enrolment needs to be analysed carefully.   When they were asked how they arrived at the decision to
join a particular union rather than another, all the women who were
interviewed on these estates answered to the effect that they had
followed the example or advice of a male.   None of them had any
real knowledge of the options that were open to them or the
differences that existed from union to union and none had been
prepared to make an independent decision.   The choice they made
was that of the husband, the superintendent, or the eldest male in
the family;   what is more, this was to such an extent an established
pattern that young women were in many instances not even consulted
but were automatically placed in the union chosen by their parents
or by their husband or brother.   In the case of the Sinhalese, who
had no other family members working on the estates, they followed
the majority or else took the advice of the thalavar or the superintendent.

Secondly, once these women had actually joined the union, they had very little interest in participating in its activities. In many cases the women were not even sure how much they paid by way of union dues.[3]   For them unions were essentially a male domain; just as men ran the family and the estate organisation, it was simply accepted that they should run the trade union movement and indeed run anything of importance within their community and that these were matters of leadership in which women should not intrude. The mechanics of their interest articulation was basically the following: if women had a problem they would speak to their husbands and try to convince them of it; the latter would then talk to the thalavar about the problem.   Often these were "women's" problems where men were reticent, where they felt uncomfortable raising or pushing what seemed to them to be embarrassing "minor problems" or unnecessary trouble.   The women had no real assurance of how their case would be put or whether complaints would be taken up at higher levels.   The men could always claim that they had raised the question, and there was very little that the women could do about it.

Those women who had broken away from the traditional norms of their own community (for example through inter-communal or inter-caste marriages or else for reasons of economic distress) appeared to be more concerned with knowing and asserting their union rights, in part at least because economic issues were more crucial to them. And yet, if only because of the break with traditional values that they had made, the protests they made were caricatured and made fun of by other women.

Thirdly, the point must be emphasised that the hierarchy of union officials is still almost entirely comprised of men. Jayaraman has suggested that there may be an element of caste in trade union structures.   It is his contention that:[4]

> the common interests as labourers are not always a uniting
> force for it is seen that in many estates the management is
> able to introduce cleavages among labourers on the basis of
> certain traditional ties such as ethnic, caste and kinship
> affiliations.   Further, the establishment of a trade union
> in itself, by giving relative importance to one or the other
> numerically important caste groups in the control of trade
> union, creates cleavages on the basis of caste ties.

Just how important this is today is difficult to assess, but it is
clear that there are divisions of various kinds amongst the workers.
The plantation workers are not a homogenous body but for all of this
trade union organisation tends to maintain a solid front of traditional attitudes as far as the women are concerned and this makes
more difficult the possibility of female expression. Given the
strengths of these feelings within the estate community, it would
be perhaps strange if there were no bias against women. Indeed,
while the situation appears to have changed very little over the
years, there are now a few thalavis (female union representatives).
They too tend to follow the established pattern of leadership within
their society and they find it hard to adopt an independent stand
even if (and this is in practice rarely the case) they recognise
the particular needs of women. More generally, it would appear to
be the case that they see themselves (and in turn are seen) as union
representatives who happen to be women and who, if they are to be
accepted and prove themselves, interpret trade union problems the
same way as the men.

Clearly, this is a problem that is rooted as much in the nature
of the society as in the nature of the unions. But the structure
is that women's grievances are not articulated forcefully and that
as a result little has in practice been achieved to overcome the
particular problems of female labour. When women were asked what
the union had done for them, their almost unanimous response was
that the unions had done nothing at all for them as women.[5] It was
not that the unions were unaware of or showed no interest in their
problems, it was that the women had seen very little by way of
practical gains and that they no longer believed in the promises
made. The fact that women were rarely consulted on union matters
meant that decisions could even be taken against their interests.
For example, the normal practice on the estates had been to issue
foodstuffs as an advance on that wage that is due at the end of
the month. On several estates the unions demanded cash in lieu of
kind on grounds that the food that was offered was of very poor
quality and that in fact they were given an inadequate range of
choice. Since the men did the shopping this was perhaps an issue
that did concern them and cash advances were made. On others,
however, the superintendents refused to comply until they had an
assurance that the women agreed. And the women did not agree.
The women saw the problem in a different perspective; they were

afraid that the men would spend the money on things other than food and that in practice the net result of this change in policy would be that it would be that much more difficult to feed their families. When this was pointed out firmly by the women the demand for cash was dropped.

Together these various factors serve to explain why trade union activities do not work as efficient channels for women to air their problems and do not bring pressure to bear on the estate management to improve their position. There are indications that at the highest levels within the union hierarchy there is an aware-ness of this problem and an interest in change, but if only because of the underlying ideology and attitudes towards women within these communities it is not easy to institute change at the grassroots level. How successful they will be remains to be seen.

Most women do take some pride in the fact that there are unions and that they belong to these unions, particularly the older ones such as the Ceylon Workers Congress. Male dominance charac-terises unions in many parts of the world, reflecting deep-rooted historical and cultural factors. Indeed the very values and sexual division of labour that characterised plantation organisation from early days are reflected in the organisation of the labour force. Women are in a subordinate situation in the wider society and if only for that reason in any powerful body, such as the trade unions, their participation is weak. Nevertheless, the trade unions remain one avenue for change that is open to them.

---

[1] This applies mainly to the tea and rubber plantations. Research has shown that most of the coconut estate workers do not belong to any trade union. This could be related to the peculiar labour requirements of the coconut plantation; it needs relatively less labour, except in certain peak periods where extra casual labour is employed. Such a pattern obviously hinders organisation among the labour. During the field work a few attempts at organising the labour were observed but nothing substantial had got off the ground.

[2] Collective bargaining problems and practices on plantations and the exercise of trade union rights (International Labour Organisation, Committee on Work on Plantations, Seventh Session, Geneva, 1976), Report II, p. 27.

[3] Unsatisfactory as these factors are, it is useful to keep them in perspective. It is not so long ago that one could have recorded similar circumstances surrounding the enrolment of women

and girls in the trade unions of some industrialised countries; and
it is certainly not unknown particularly in the rural unions of the
developing countries, for male workers to also be unaware of the
amount they pay in union dues.

[4] R. Jayaraman: <u>Caste continuities in Ceylon: A study of the</u>
<u>social structure of three tea plantations</u> (Bombay, Popular Prakashan
Press, 1975), p. 121.

[5] On one estate the women asked the <u>thalavar</u> to see if they
could be granted leave when their children were sick: nothing was
done.   One widow who had suddenly found herself left with five
children approached the thalavar to see if she could get some form
of assistance: nothing was done.   What the unions did achieve was
only temporary: sometimes the water came on for two or three days,
and then went off.

Chapter 8

POSSIBLE AREAS FOR AMELIORATIVE ACTION

Based on the analyses contained in the previous chapters, a
number of issues would seem to stand out as particularly important
areas warranting more careful attention on the part of the management of the nationalised Sri Lankan estates and of policy-makers.

1. The first point which needs to be stressed in this respect
is the fundamental one that any strategy concerned with improving
the situation of plantation labour has to pay specific attention to
the situation of women. The indications are that this dimension
is generally lacking, and that many of the policies which are implemented work against the particular interests of women and are policies with which women workers disagree. Such is the importance
of these women numerically and of their tasks, that this is an over-
sight that is likely in time to work against the interests of the
plantation itself.

2. Secondly, with regard to the income and wage rates of plantation workers, several issues stand out as in need of special attention:

(a) There is need for a careful investigation to be carried
     out into the economics of a shift towards equal wages for work
     of equal value. (At the moment there even exists unequal wages
     for the same work depending on if it is done by a man or woman.)
     The importance of such a policy is recognised amongst both trade
     unionists and estate superintendents, but as yet the necessary
     policy measures have not been adequately worked through to
     find ways in which they could be viably introduced.

(b) There is a serious need for more consideration to be given
     to the question of the minimum wage. As we have noted, there
     are still wide variations in the availability of work from
     month to month, workers continue to be very vulnerable in times
     of ill health, and wages are strongly influenced by the size
     of the harvest. The idea of a fixed monthly wage for all
     registered workers warrants more thought, although serious
     research will be required to find ways of making it feasible
     in the light of the current problems of profitability within
     the estate sector.

(c) A third issue relates much more to management methods, and
it is concerned with incentives.   There is reason to believe
that the setting of work norms on tea, and to some extent on
rubber estates are not adjusted as frequently as is needed,
sometimes remaining fixed for very long periods of time (sometimes even for many months at a time).   Not only does this
reduce the possibility of workers augmenting their income, but
it reduces the crop intake by removing incentives, and could
well affect the profitability of certain estates.   This particularly affects the income of women because it is they who pick
the tea and tap the rubber.

(d) Closely related to this is the fact that the declining overkilo" rate, as outlined in the text, is often in practice quite
unrealistic and that it needs to be revised if it is to provide
any meaningful incentive.   These two points (points (c) and
(d)) concerning management methods could very effectively be
considered together.

(e) Finally, concerning the payment of wages, management should
wherever possible try to ensure that time and opportunity are
made available for women to collect their own pay so that they
are in a better position to have some control over it.   Much
would be gained by implementing the general rule that a worker
is paid directly for her or his work, and not some representative acting on their behalf.

3.   On the matter of medical and welfare facilities a number
of issues can again be raised:

(a) Firstly, having examined the existing situation, it would
seem important that more attention should be given to the rights
of casual workers.   Many of these people are classified as
"casual", particularly on coconut estates, because of the labour
requirements of the particular crop.   They are nevertheless
part of the regular labour force and (where these are available)
they should be eligible for the welfare and other facilities
open to registered workers.

(b) There is no doubt at all that housing conditions pose a
very serious problem, and one which is made considerably worse
by sanitary arrangements and the inadequate water supplies.
In the latter regard the efforts that have been made in the
past have often been thwarted by consistent misuse, but no one

who visits the average estate line can in any way doubt that
this is a problem which has to be tackled, and one for which
a solution has to be found.   Again, these are problems which
particularly affect the estate women.

(c)   Nursing mothers should also wherever possible be given more
time to care for their children than they are in the working
arrangements of most estates.   This could be achieved through
rearrangement or a shortening of the working day.   Given the
distances that are involved, the time that is allowed is often
unrealistic and even that is not implemented rigorously throughout the plantation as an accepted rule.   More careful consideration needs to be given to this.

(d)   Much work has recently been done under the auspices of
UNICEF to upgrade the crèches that are provided on the estates.
However, by no means every estate has been able to take advantage of this, and many crèches continue to be in a very poor
condition.   Furthermore, providing the crèche only goes part
of the way towards solving the problem.   It would be extremely
useful if someone were to organise the collection of the children from homes or from the crèche.   There are many instances
where the distances involved more or less preclude the possibility of the woman using the crèche and still feeding her
child, and in a great many other instances it is such that it
places a considerable burden upon the woman to collect and
return the child in the time that is allotted.

(e)   Fifthly, serious and careful attention needs to be given
to the education that is received by children in general and
by girls in particular in the estate schools.   It seems reasonable to suggest that there be some monitoring of their attendance
in order to bring the scale and the nature of this problem
into clearer perspective, and efforts be made to ensure
that they do receive a complete education.   This may in practice require some revision of current thinking with regard to
crèche, medical and other welfare facilities, and to non-estate
incomes and employment.

Again it would be invaluable for these women if the estate
could arrange in one way or another for the collection of children to and from schools.

(f) With regard to medical facilities, questions can be raised
concerning the uniformity of the facilities which are being
offered on different estates and the adequacy and availability
of transport arrangements for those who are in need of special
attention. Family planning programmes should also pay more
attention to other forms of contraception besides tubectomy
and vasectomy, and sufficient time should be allowed before
these operations for welfare officers to discuss with the
patients and to allay some of the fears and worries that they
are likely to have. Arrangements should also be made to ensure
that it is the women who receive the maternity benefits.

There are serious grounds for believing that women should be
allocated somewhat lighter tasks in the period immediately
after tubectomy.

(g) Some attempt should also be made wherever possible to moni-
tor the violence occurring on estates and to devise means of
securing the women protection in one form or another - at least
in the most severe cases there should be some place or some
person to whom they have recourse.

4. With regard to the repatriation of workers to India, the
policy of giving the Provident Fund and other entitlements of the
whole family to the man often results in serious hardships for women.
Much might well be done to improve their position if documentation
and even monies were given to each worker individually as a matter
of right.

5. In the long run an important factor in ensuring the
consideration of women in the formulation and implementation of policy
is potentially at least, the trade union movement. It seems important that the interests and needs of women are aired more in these
circles. In this regard a number of issues stand out as particularly important:

(a) Firstly, trade union meetings at the estate level could
be organised in such a way that women can attend them. There
is an argument that this is not possible because they have to
look after the children and the household; they have not
generally come up with other arrangements.

(b) At these meetings there can be a concerted effort to
encourage women to air their views and to voice their grievances.

(c)   Given the inhibitions that prevail in the communications between men and women, it is unlikely that the women would be very vocal in front of a male audience.   It would be constructive, therefore, if separate women's units within existing trade unions were established, where the leadership would be female, and where the women could speak out in larger meetings through their representatives who could speak out in the knowledge that the others were behind them.   These groups could also be granted a certain autonomy and encouraged to understand more effectively their role in the plantation system and the issues which were at stake for them as women.

(d)   In all these cases, there is a need for workers' education concerning the needs of women.   Much hinges on the attitudes adopted by the trade union leadership and their enthusiasm in bettering the situation.

These must be seen as tentative suggestions.   The position of women workers on the Sri Lankan plantations is in many ways a difficult one.   Viewed over-all, there is clearly a need for radical changes, and the struggle to bring about change will often be hard. Finally, therefore, there can be an attempt to link them with the political activities of women in other parts of the world, to make their case known and to gain for them additional support, and to make possible the exchange of views, experiences and ideas.

BIBLIOGRAPHY

Books and articles

H.C. Abell: "Labour availability", in CIDA/Government of Sri Lanka: The tea master plan study (Position paper No. 4, Colombo, 1978).

A.H. Adamson: Sugar without slaves: The political economy of British Guyana 1838-1904 (New Haven and London, Yale University Press, 1978).

A.C.L. Ameer Ali: "Rice and irrigation in 19th century Sri Lanka", in The Ceylon Historical Journal (Dehiwala), Vol. XXV, Nos. 1-4, Oct. 1978.

M. d'Auberteuil: Considerations sur l'état present de la colonie française de St. Dominique (Paris, 1776), vol. 2.

G. Beckford: Persistent poverty (London, Oxford University Press, 1972).

A. Beteille: Caste, class and power (Berkeley, University of California Press, 1971).

E. Bond: The state of tea (Colombo, 1974).

Ceylon Directory (for various years) (Colombo, A.M. and J. Ferguson).

Collective bargaining problems and practice on plantations and the exercise of trade union rights. Report by the Committee on Work on Plantations, International Labour Office (Geneva, International Labour Office, 1976) Seventh Session, Report II.

G. Corea: The instability of an export economy (Colombo, Marga Institute, 1975).

M. Cranton: Searching for the invisible man: slaves and plantation life in Jamaica (Cambridge (Massachusetts) and London, Harvard University Press, 1978).

W. Dean: Rio Claro: a Brazilian plantation system 1820-1920 (Stanford, Stanford University Press, 1976).

N. Deerr: The history of sugar (London, Chapman and Hall, 1950).

I.H. van den Driesen: "Coffee cultivation in Ceylon", in The Ceylon Historical Journal (Dehiwala) 1954.

I.H. van den Driesen: "Plantation agriculture and land sales policy in Ceylon: the first phase 1836-1886" (Part I), in University of Ceylon Review (Colombo), Volume XIV, No. 1, Jan. 1956.

J. Ferguson: Ceylon in the jubilee year (London 1887).

D.M. Forrest: A hundred years of Ceylon tea (London, Chatto and Windus, 1967.

D. Ghai, A. Khan, E. Lee and S. Radwan (eds.): Agrarian systems and rural development (London, The Macmillan Press Ltd., 1979).

L. Green: The planter's book of caste and custom (Colombo, The Times of Ceylon Company Ltd., and London, Blackfriars House, 1925).

S.M. Greenfield: "Slavery and the plantation in the New World", in the Journal of Inter-American Studies (Gainsville, University of Miami), Volume II, No. 1, 1969.

R. Guerra y Sánchez: Sugar and society in the Caribbean: an economic history of Cuban agriculture (English translation) (New Haven and London, Yale University Press, 1964).

G.M. Hall: Social control in slave plantation societies (Baltimore and London, Johns Hopkins University Press, 1971).

H.W. Hutchinson: "The transformation of Brazilian plantation society", in Journal of Inter-American Studies (Gainsville, University of Miami), Vol. III, No. 2, Apr. 1961.

J.M. Hutton: Caste in India (London, Oxford University Press, 1963).

R. Jayaraman: Caste continuities in Ceylon: a study of the social structure of three tea plantations (Bombay, Popular Prakashan Press, 1975).

K.V. Jayawardena: The rise of the labour movement in Ceylon (Durham (North Carolina), Duke University Press, 1972).

R. Kearney: Trade unions and politics in Ceylon (New Delhi, Thomson Press (India) Ltd., and Berkeley, University of California Press, 1971).

R. Knox: An historical relation of Ceylon (Glasgow, James MacLehose and Sons, 1911).

M. Kossak: "Common aspects and distinctive features in colonial Latin America", in Science and Society (New York, John Jay College), Vol. XXXVII, Spring No. 1, 1973.

Land reform and the development of coconut lands, a study prepared by the Agrarian Research and Training Institute (Colombo, 1977).

E.R. Leach (ed.): Aspects of caste in South India, Ceylon and North West Pakistan (Cambridge, Cambridge University Press, 1960).

E.R. Leach: Pul Eliya - a village in Ceylon: a study of land tenure and kinship (Cambridge, Cambridge University Press, 1961).

E.O. von Lippmann: História do açucar (2 volumes) (Rio de Janeiro, Instituto do Açucar e Alcool, 1942).

Matching employment opportunities and expectations - a programme of action for Ceylon. The Report of an inter-agency team organised by the International Labour Office (Geneva, ILO, 1971).

A.C. Meyer: Caste and kinship in Central India (London, Routledge and Kegan Paul, 1960).

L. de Mel: The evolution of industrial relations in Ceylon with special reference to the plantations (Geneva, ILO, 1972).

P.D. Millie: Thirty years ago: reminiscences of the early days of coffee planting in Ceylon (Colombo, A.M. and J. Ferguson, 1878).

B.M. Morrison, M.P. Moore and M.U. Ishar Lebbe (eds.): The disintegrating village: social change in Sri Lanka (Colombo, Lake House Investments, 1979).

K.P. Mukerjee: "The Ceylon wages board", in The Ceylon Economist (Colombo) Vol. I, No. 2, 1950.

S.E.N. Nicholas: Estate labour and legal guide (Colombo, C.A.P. Press, 1927).

G. Obeyesekere: Land tenure in village Ceylon (Cambridge, Cambridge University Press, 1967).

J. Paige: Agrarian revolution - social movements and export agriculture in the underdeveloped world (New York, Free Press, 1975).

B.L. Panditaratne and S. Selvanayagani: "The demography of Ceylon - an introductory survey", in K.M. de Silva (ed.): University of Ceylon History of Ceylon (Colombo, University of Ceylon, Press Board, 1973).

O. Patterson: The sociology of slavery: an analysis of the origins, development and structure of Negro slave society in Jamaica (London, Reading and Fakenham, Macgibbon and Kee, 1967).

A.M.S. Perara: "The tea industry of Sri Lanka", in Marga (Colombo), Tea, Special Issue, Vol. 3, No. 4, 1976.

R. Percival: An account of the island of Ceylon (London, 1803).

G.H. Pieris: "Ceylon's prospects in the world rubber market", in The Ceylon Journal of Historical and Social Studies (Peradeniya), Vol. 9, No. 2, July-Dec. 1966.

G.H. Pieris: "Land reform and agrarian change in Sri Lanka", in Modern Asian Studies (Cambridge and New York) Vol. 12, No. 4, 1978.

R. Pieris: Sinhalese social organisation - the Kandyan period (Colombo, Ceylon University Press, 1956).

Plantations systems of the New World. Papers and discussion summaries of the seminar held in San Juan Puerto Rio (Washington D.C., Pan American Union and Research Institute for the Study of Man, 1957).

Plantation workers: conditions of work and standards of living. Studies and Reports, New Series, No. 69 (Geneva, ILO, 1966).

J. Reis: "Abolition and the economics of slave-holdings in northeast Brazil", in Boletín de Estudios Latinoamericanos y del Caribe (Amsterdam, CEDLA, No. 17, Dec. 1974).

Report on the survey of expatriates from Sri Lanka 1980 (Madras Centre for Research on the New International Economic Order 1980).

P. Richards: Comment on Iseman: "basic needs: the case of Sri Lanka", in World Development (Oxford) Vol. 9, No. 2, 1981.

P. Richards: Employment and unemployment in Ceylon (Paris, Organisation for Economic Co-operation and Development, 1971).

M. Roberts: "The master-servant laws of 1841 and the 1860s and
immigrant labour in Ceylon", in The Ceylon Journal of Historical
and Social Studies (Peradeniya), Vol. 8, 1965.

M. Roberts and L.A. Wickremeratne: "Export agriculture in the nine-
teenth century", in K.M. de Silva (eds.): University of Ceylon
History of Ceylon (Colombo, University of Ceylon Press Board, 1973),
Vol. III.

M. Roberts (ed.): Collective identities, nationalisms and protest
in modern Sri Lanka (Colombo, Marga Institute, 1979).

W. Sabonadiere: The coffee planter of Ceylon (Colombo, Mees, J.P.
Green and Co., 1866).

J.A. Saco: Historia de la esclavidud de la raza africana en el nuevo
mundo (Barcelona, 1879).

V. Samaraweera: "Economic and social developments under the British",
in K.M. de Silva (ed.): University of Ceylon History of Ceylon
(Colombo, University of Ceylon Press Board, 1973), Vol. III.

C.D. Scott: Machetes, machines and agrarian reform: the political
economy of technical choice in the Peruvian sugar industry, 1954-1974
(Norwich, School of Development Studies, University of East Anglia,
1979).

N. Shanmugaratnam: "Impact of plantation economy and colonial policy
on Sri Lankan peasantry", in Economic and Political Weekly 17 Jan.
1981.

K.M. de Silva: "Resistance movements in nineteenth century Sri Lanka",
in M. Roberts (ed.): Collective identities, nationalisms and protest
in modern Sri Lanka (Colombo, Marga Institute, 1979).

K.M. de Silva (ed.): University of Ceylon History of Ceylon (Colombo,
Univeristy of Ceylon Press Board, 1973), Vol. III.

K.T. de Silva: "The demise of Kandyan feudalism", in B.M. Morrison,
M.P. Moore and M.U. Ishak Lebbe (eds.): The disintegrating village:
social change in Sri Lanka (Colombo, Lake House Investments, 1979).

R.T. Smith: "Family structure and plantation systems in the new
world", in Plantation systems of the New World (Washington D.C.,
Pan American Union and Research Institute for the Study of Man, 1959).

D.R. Snodgrass: Ceylon: an export economy in transition (Homewood,
Illinois, Richard D. Irwin, Inc. for the Economic Growth Centre,
Yale University, 1966).

M.N. Srinivas: Religion and society among the Coorgs of South India
(Oxford, Clarendon Press, 1952).

M.N. Srinivas: Caste in modern India and other essays (London, Asia
Publishing House, 1962).

Survey of rural indebtedness (Colombo, Central Bank of Ceylon, 1969).

W.M. Talakaratne: "Rural indebtedness in Ceylon", in Ceylon Economist (Colombo), Vol. 4, No. 2, 1958).

C. Thomas: "Agrarian change in a plantation economy: the case of Guyana", in D. Ghai, A. Khan, E. Lee and S. Radwan (eds.): Agrarian systems and rural development (London, The Macmillan Press Ltd., 1979).

Times of Ceylon tea supplement to mark the Ceylon tea century (Colombo 1967).

N.E. Weerasooria: Ceylon and her people (Colombo, Lake House Investments, 1970).

J.A. Weller: The east Indian indenture in Trinidad (Rio Piedras: Institute of Caribbean Studies, University of Puerto Rico, 1968).

L.A. Wickremeratne: "The development of transportation in Ceylon 1800-1947", in K.D. de Silva (ed.): University of Ceylon History of Ceylon (Colombo, University of Ceylon Press Board, 1973), Vol. III.

W.A. Wiswa Warnapala: Civil Service administration in Ceylon (Colombo, Department of Cultural Affairs, 1974).

Unpublished Works

A.C.L. Ameer Ali: Peasant agriculture in Ceylon 1833-1893, M. Phil. Thesis, University of London, 1970.

D. Dunham: Land, plantations and peasants in Sri Lankan development: the period prior to 1900, Institute of Social Studies, The Hague, 1980.

D. Dunham: Government policy towards peasants and towards colonisation: the period up to 1931, Institute of Social Studies, The Hague, 1980.

N. Gunasinghe: Changing socio-economic relations in the Kandyan countryside, Ph.D. Thesis, Univeristy of Sussex, 1980.

L. Jayawardena: The supply of Sinhalese labour to Ceylon plantations (1830-1930), Ph.D. Thesis, University of Cambridge, 1963.

R.E. Reddock: Women and slavery: A feminist perspective, Institute of Social Studies, The Hague, 1980.

N. Shanmugaratnam: A study of joint-farming systems, Ph.D. Thesis, University of Colombo 1979.

Official Publications

Address of the President: To the directors and planters of the Janatha Estates Development Board and Sri Lanka State Plantations Corporation (Colombo 1980).

Administration Reports (Colombo, Government of Ceylon), published annually.

Bulletin of the Central Bank of Ceylon (Colombo, Central Bank of Ceylon), published monthly.

Census of India (Madras 1931).

"Cooly lines on Ceylon estates", in Legislative Council Debates (Colombo, Sri Lanka National Archives, 24 Feb. 1927).

Despatches (official correspondence between the Governor and the Secretary of State) (Colombo, Sri Lanka National Archives).

"District Hospitality Mortality Commission", in Sessional Papers No. II of 1893 (Colombo 1893).

Economic and social development of Ceylon: a survey presented to the Parliament by the Minister of Finance, M.D. Jayawardane (Colombo 1955).

"History of finance", Budget speech for 1980 by the Minister of Finance, R. de Mel, in National State Assembly Debates (Colombo, 14 Nov. 1979).

Report and proceedings of the Labour Commission headed by Sir Hugh Clifford (Colombo, 1908)

Report of the Commission of inquiry on agency houses and brokering firms, Sessional Paper No. XII of 1974 (Colombo 1974).

Report of the Coconut Commission, Sessional Paper No. XII of 1949 (Colombo, 1949).

Report of a Commission to inquire into the conditions of immigrant Tamil labourers in the planting districts of Sabaragamuwa (Colombo, 1916).

Report of a Commission on immigration into Ceylon in Sessional Papers No. III of 1938 (Colombo, 1938).

Report of the Commission on the rubber industry in Ceylon in Sessional Papers XVIII of 1947 (Colombo, 1947).

Report on unemployment in Ceylon, in Sessional Papers No. VII of 1937 (Colombo, 1937).

Report of the Tea Commission, in Sessional Papers No. XVIII of 1968 (Colombo, 1968).

Report of the Kandyan Peasantry Commission, in Sessional Papers No. XVIII of 1951 (Colombo, 1951).

Service for children in the estate areas (Colombo, UNICEF, n.d.) (the programme started in 1979).

Sri Lanka Gazette, May Day Supplement (Colombo, Ministry of Labour, 1979).

Sri Lanka Nutrition Survey (Colombo, 1976).

State Council Debates (Colombo, Government of Ceylon), various volumes.

Statistical Abstract of the Democratic Socialist Republic of Sri Lanka 1977 (Colombo, 1977).

"The law relating to Indian labourers", in <u>Legislative Council Debates</u> (Colombo, 1926).

<u>The socio-economic survey of Ceylon 1969-1970</u> (Colombo, Department of Census and Statistics, 1970).

<u>Twenty-five years of labour progress</u> (Colombo, Department of Labour, 1948).